Praise for *The Ghosts Who Travel with Me*

"Charming, wry, and elliptical. *The Ghosts Who Travel with Me* takes readers on a humorous and deeply nostalgic tour of America, and plumbs the depths of 'Generation Jones.' Vastly entertaining."

—Diana Abu-Jaber, author of *The Language of Baklava* and *Birds of Paradise*

"I can't think of a wiser, craftier, kinder travel companion than Allison Green. Yet for as much fun as I had reading *The Ghosts Who Travel with Me*, I also found myself challenged and provoked and asked to grapple with the legacies of my own ancestors, literary and otherwise. *The Ghosts Who Travel with Me* will keep you thinking, and feeling, long after you turn the last page."

—Joe Wilkins, winner of the 2014 GLCA New Writers Award for *The Mountain and the Fathers*

"*Ghosts* is so seamlessly put together that it's hard to point to the concrete moments to explain just why I found it so lovely. It's an ephemeral effect, the words and pages gently building until you suddenly find yourself transported back to the moment that you, too, fell in love with an author for nothing more than their words on the pages. For those us of who call ourselves readers, our relationship with books is something that can feel religious; *The Ghosts Who Travel with Me* is a missive for the true believers. Green's love-letter to the first author she fell in love with is a memoir that will resonate with anyone who has finished a book and then sighed that the journey had to end."

—Mensah Demary, *Four Culture*

The Ghosts Who Travel with Me

The Ghosts Who Travel with Me

A Literary Pilgrimage through Brautigan's America

Allison Green

Ooligan
PRESS

The Ghosts Who Travel with Me: A Literary Pilgrimage through Brautigan's America
© 2015 Allison Green

ISBN 978-1-932010-77-0

Ooligan Press
Portland State University
Post Office Box 751, Portland, Oregon 97207
503.725.9748
ooligan@ooliganpress.pdx.edu
http://ooligan.pdx.edu

Library of Congress Cataloging-in-Publication Data

Green, Allison.
   The ghosts who travel with me : a literary pilgrimage through Brautigan's America / Allison Green.
     pages cm
   ISBN 978-1-932010-77-0
   1. Green, Allison. 2. Women authors, American--20th century--Biography. 3. Women and literature--United States--History--20th century. 4. Brautigan, Richard--Influence. 5. Literary landmarks--United States. 6. Feminism and literature--United States--History--20th century. I. Title.
   PS3557.R3587Z46 2015
   813'.54--DC23
   [B]
                              2015001315

Cover design by Ryan Brewer & Meaghan Corwin
Interior design by Zach Eggemeyer

Full credits located on page 169.

Printed in the United States of America

For Arline, mi compañera

CONTENTS

The
Girl
from
Idaho

A Long, Slow Drive

"Why Idaho?" The barista set cups on saucers and next to them tiny silver spoons.

I said, "Why not Idaho?"

My partner Arline and I planned to drive from Seattle to Boise in one day, a journey that MapQuest said would take eight hours and twenty-three minutes. We had dropped our black lab off with my parents and stopped at a coffeehouse on our way out of town.

The barista told us, in a confessional rush, that she was fifth-generation Idaho. Her father had been in the legislature so she'd lived half the year in Hope and half the year in Boise. Did we know where Coeur d'Alene was? I did. And north of that Sandpoint? If we went east from there we'd get to Hope. A little town.

We weren't going to Coeur d'Alene, I said, or anywhere in northern Idaho. We were going to Boise and then up into the Sawtooth Mountains. I didn't say we were on a literary pilgrimage.

She made perfect cream tulips on the surface of our coffee. "Don't worry about the Aryan Nations," she said, sliding the cups across the counter. "It's better now. Believe me, I was a little dyke. I stole the next-door neighbor's wife. And they didn't do anything. Oh, they drove down our driveway one night, took a long, slow drive by our house. But that's all."

Arline and I took our dyke selves back to the car. I brushed scone crumbs off my shirt.

Arline said, "She doesn't live in Idaho anymore. She lives here."

"It's just for a week," I said. "One week in Idaho." I got on Interstate 90 and headed east.

I first heard the term "Generation Jones" when Barack Obama was running for president. Coined by sociologist Jonathan Pontell, it refers to those of us born between the mid-1950s and mid-1960s. He says that because we were born into idealism but grew up in the cynical 1970s, we're jonesing for something more but not sure what it is. My earliest hippie memory is in Seattle's Volunteer Park; a young woman paints a butterfly on my arm while my parents watch from a picnic blanket. I look up at the woman's beatific smile, her silky hair, and then I look down, craning to see the pink and purple butterfly near my smallpox vaccination scar. The young woman takes my hand and leads me to the dancing circle. I'm the only child among the flower children.

Being born in 1963 meant I was lumped in with the baby boomers but too young to stay at the party; my parents made me go home for a nap. I wasn't old enough to hop a bus to Woodstock or find my way to Haight-Ashbury when it was still sweet. Instead, I danced in the living room to the 5th Dimension's "Age of Aquarius" and watched *Laugh-In* on Monday nights. When I grew up, I knew, a bus would take me someplace magical.

A nostalgia for times missed seeped through my adolescence. Protesting the return of draft registration in the late 1970s was not as dramatic as protesting the war. At fourteen I was playing my guitar and singing Joni Mitchell's "Circle Game" on the street in the University District when a man with long hair gave me a look that said: Sorry, you missed it. I never played "Circle Game" on the street again.

My mother, who was born in 1940, watched the college freshmen doing the Twist; she and the other seniors looked on in bewilderment. She has never once expressed regret for being "too old" for flower power. One of my favorite pictures of her is at a protest where she is pregnant with me and holding a sign that says "ban the bomb"; she was marching for peace when the flower children were walking to school with their Lone Ranger lunch boxes.

So there, I say to you older baby boomers; so there: my mother and I straddle your pig-in-a-python generation; we've got you surrounded. Except that everything you had, I wanted; everything you did, I wanted to do, for years and years and years.

A Nostalgic Morning

Easter morning, six months before we leave for Idaho. Arline and I are drinking coffee and reading *The New York Times* while Pogo snores beneath the dining room table. I'm not wearing tie-dye or Birkenstocks; my obsession with sixties culture is long gone. The oldest boomers are seventeen years older than me, and even if sixty is the new fifty, that still makes me seventeen years younger. Finally, I've got something on them.

I read in the travel section about someone's pilgrimage to Mexico to find the spirit of Ken Kesey. A sidebar lists several other psychedelic authors whose trips one might retrace: William Burroughs in Morocco, Jack Kerouac in San Francisco, Richard Brautigan in Idaho. Brautigan's trip became the novel *Trout Fishing in America*. People still remember that old book?

Because it's spring break and I don't have any English comp papers to grade, I have the luxury of going upstairs to our attic and looking for the book on our shelves. There it is, a slim pink paperback, the spine faded lighter than the cover. I haven't opened that cover in years, but now I turn to the title page, where the letters of *Trout Fishing in America* form an arc: a spray of water or a fishing pole and line. I sit on the top step of the staircase and page through the book. The text looks as if it's been typed on a typewriter: the title, mentioned in the first chapter, is underlined, not italicized, and the chapter titles are in all caps. The book looks handmade, as if Brautigan typed his musings in one draft, Xeroxed and stapled them, and handed them out on a San Francisco street corner.

The first chapter, all of two pages, describes the cover photograph: San Francisco's Washington Square, with its Benjamin Franklin statue and a historically significant cypress tree.

I turn back to the cover. There's the Benjamin Franklin statue, all right, and what might be the cypress tree. But there are also two people on the cover: Brautigan in a peacoat and a woman in a cape and granny glasses whose style would have struck me as the height of sophistication when I first read the book. Who is she? Her name isn't with the photographer's on the copyright page. It isn't on the back cover. And she's never mentioned in Brautigan's own description of the cover. Of course not. The woman is the muse. Not worth a mention. If there was one thing that ruined hippie culture for me, it was realizing how sexist it was. All those communes, and the women were still stuck with the dishes.

I sit on the top stair in our attic, under the skylight, rubbing my thumb over the creases in what was once a glossy cover. I look up at the slot in the bookshelf where the book lives. As a teenager I bought every Brautigan book available. At some point I got rid of all of them but this one. Why did I keep it? I bought my Brautigan books at Shorey's, a used bookstore that took up several floors of an old building in downtown Seattle. On rainy days the windows would be open, bringing in the smell of the waterfront and the sound of cars on slick streets. The radiators blasted, too hot, as I poked through the shelves and piles of books on the floor, on chairs, on windowsills. Often no one was there but me. The vastness of the collection would have been overwhelming, but I had my list of Brautigan books to find. The books were never more than a dollar or two, and that's how I spent most of my allowance.

When, years later, I had to get rid of most of my books to move east, I must have decided that *Trout Fishing in America* would be the one to represent all that I had read and loved as a teenager. But who had that girl been? And did she notice that the woman on the cover had no name?

I could slide the book back onto the shelf and leave it there. But something makes me put it on my nightstand to read again. And then I go to my desk and google Brautigan and find something called the Brautigan archives. I learn the woman's name: Michaela Clark LeGrand.

This is what happened to late baby boomer girls: they fell in love with writers like Brautigan. Some of you are swooning: Brautigan! I loved *Trout Fishing in America*/*In Watermelon Sugar*/that poem about the turd on the garbage can lid. You can see, through a haze of nostalgic pot smoke, the paperback on the ledge of your dorm window, the one passed from friend to friend. You remember your lover reading it aloud—before sex to get your attention, afterwards to keep the glow glowing.

Some of you are turning up your noses at the writer who never hit Ginsberg quality (or Kerouac or Tom Wolfe or whatever icon you were drooling over in 1967, when *Trout Fishing in America* was published; I was only four that year and not long past a different kind of drooling). Some of you weren't reading white males at all at the time, dead or alive. Some of you, my late boomer *confrères* and those born even later, don't have a clue who I'm talking about.

The first hundred miles of our Idaho trip, from Seattle to Ellensburg, were as familiar as my pulse. When I was growing up, my father's parents lived in a Seattle suburb and my mother's parents lived in Spokane, and Interstate 90 between them was the central artery of our family's heart. We'd leave Seattle through the I-90 tunnel, skim across the surface of Lake Washington, drive through the wealthy eastside suburbs, and wind our way up into the foothills of the Cascades and over Snoqualmie Pass. The temperature could drop twenty, thirty degrees in the hour it took to ascend from sea level to summit. In August, this could be refreshing; in February, it was almost mystical how quickly dreary rain turned to glittery snow.

This was September, and the sky was a tight blue skin over the Cascade peaks. The car strained up to the pass and flew down the other side. The air on the eastern slopes was hot and dry, the fields parched if they weren't irrigated. We had our traveling CDs in a black zippered case, and the one in the player was Lucinda Williams. She was singing her long, loping phrases. "Come out west and see," she sang just as we left the Seattle kind of west—moss and rain, ferries and gulls—and drove into the west of scrub and heat and blue lakes. This trip wasn't only a literary pilgrimage; it was our last bit of summer before returning to work at the community college where we both taught. Going over the pass into Eastern Washington felt like stretching our wings one last September moment.

by a sister who lived near Seattle, and she had toured places like San Francisco and New York. But she didn't visit Pend Oreille County of Eastern Washington until I dragged her to a family reunion there. Arline's lack of travel experience in the rural West was not due to lack of interest; she was intrigued by my ancestral homes, and she talked often of someday taking a road trip through the vast checkerboard of states. When I proposed Idaho, she was curious. She was especially interested in the Basque community in Boise, its restaurants and museum. It was only as the date of our departure drew closer that apprehension overtook curiosity.

When we first met, Arline sometimes called me "the girl from Idaho." Actually, I was born in Ohio while my parents were in graduate school, but Arline joked that she got the vowelly states mixed up. Never having been to Idaho, Arline had all those bad associations with it: Aryan Nations, rednecks, acres of rural nothingness. So calling me "the girl from Idaho" was a teasing way to put me in my place, to remind me of my unsophisticated roots. Peel back an insult and you find a wound: to be "the girl from Panama" is to be an immigrant from somewhere inconsequential to most Americans.

The problem with calling me "the girl from Idaho" was that I had barely spent any time in the state. Although cousins on my mother's side lived there, we always met them at my grandparents' lake cabin in Eastern Washington. My paternal grandparents had grown up in Idaho, but they were living in the Seattle area by the time I was born. In truth, it bothered me when Arline called me "the girl from Idaho." I had those images of Idaho in my head, too. Idaho was just a panhandle of land to pass through on the way to wilder, more beautiful Montana.

⁂

At Ellensburg, we veered onto less familiar ground, Interstate 82, which winds southeast through the "fruit bowl of the nation." Farmers here have grown cherries, apples, pears, and grapes for generations, and now the region is becoming known for its wineries. Arline looked at the map of wine-tasting rooms in the guidebook. We found one, but it turned out to be in a strip mall Scotch-taped to a farmer's field. After a couple of sips, we bought a bottle and were on our way.

We crossed into Oregon and soon were driving through my mother's birthplace, Pendleton. On other visits I'd found the hospital where she was born and bought a jacket at the woolen mills. Pendleton is known for its Round-Up, a festival of bareback riding, calf roping, steer wrestling, bull riding, and wild cow milking that draws thousands. The Round-Up was starting in a few days, but we were just passing through.

In La Grande it was time for lunch. Some years before, my brother and I had driven through La Grande on our way to Cambridge, Idaho, to see where my grandmother had been buried. We'd eaten sandwiches at a cute coffee shop downtown. But now I circled and circled the old western buildings and found nothing that matched the café in my memory. As much as I like traveling somewhere new, I have a tendency to look for exactly what I've just left behind. If La Grande had had a coffee shop exactly like the one where we'd bought coffee that morning, I would have been happy to go there. We found sandwiches at a café that wasn't as cute as the one I remembered, and we got back on the road.

Arline was driving now, and somewhere along Interstate 84 where it followed the parched brown route of the Oregon Trail, she said, "So what was it about Brautigan?"

I was thinking that it was interesting to be taking the Oregon Trail backwards, east not west, and that the ghosts of the ones who died along the way must be wondering at the whizzing of our tires. "That's what I'm trying to figure out." I told her that when I went back to my adolescent journals, after rereading *Trout Fishing in America*, I'd discovered that Brautigan appeared more than any other writer. In one entry, when I was thirteen, I'd made a list of what I would do if I knew I was dying: fall in love, learn to speak my mind, sing on a street corner, tour Europe and South America, smoke pot, and meet Brautigan. "I've done all those things but one," I said. Unfortunately, Brautigan was long gone now. But his Idaho wasn't.

We hit sprawl in Caldwell, Idaho. Traffic crept. Heat pulsed off the asphalt. Gas stations, shopping malls, auto dealers, and billboards didn't let up for over thirty miles as we skirted Nampa and Meridian. Semis and SUVs boxed in our little Honda. In Brautigan's time, there must have been a gentler way into Idaho.

But once we exited for Boise, we were charmed. A cluster of tall buildings and the white-domed capitol marked the small downtown, about ten blocks square. The flat, wide streets were perfect for strolling and bicycling. We pulled into the parking lot of the Modern Hotel and turned off the engine. It ticked in the quiet of the warm Sunday evening. We were here.

Trout Frying in America

My maternal grandmother, born in a sod house on the South Dakota prairie and raised in Montana, made sourdough pancakes with starter that had been kept alive in a mason jar for generations. Women kept on feeding it and feeding it and passing it along to their daughters, and I was the lucky child in the late 1960s who stood nose to counter and watched my grandmother pour in this and sift in that and stir briskly with a wooden spoon and ladle onto the griddle and flip when the bubbles rose to the top. I like to imagine I spread my sourdough pancakes with butter and Vermont maple syrup, but actually I knifed a big chunk of margarine out of the tub and onto my pancakes and followed this with syrup out of the plastic Aunt Jemima bottle. This was when Aunt Jemima wore that kerchief and made white America comfortable.

My grandmother could make biscuits on the counter

with no recipe and no bowl. She sifted flour and baking soda and salt into a pile, cut in the butter with a knife and fork, made a depression in the top for the eggs and milk, stirred them in, kneaded quickly, and cut out biscuits with the mouth of a tumbler. As we grandchildren grew older, we said: "Grandma, what's your recipe?" A little of this, a little of that. Until it looks right.

The menfolk cleaned the fish, and the womenfolk fried them. Although both men and women may have used frying pans on wood fires, frying pans on stoves were the tools of women. Trout were dredged in flour or cornmeal and fried, heads off or heads on, until the flesh left its state of translucence and turned opaque. Women knew without knowing the name for it that the muscles of fish are held together by collagen that dissolves quickly in the heat, leaving only the muscle fibers. Those fibers turn from pearly to tough in the time it takes to slide a paring knife under the trout's skin.

The sourdough starter was lost to me. I chose, upon my grandmother's death, a white glass chicken with a red wattle that she kept filled with pink and white mints. It doesn't replace her pancakes or her biscuits or her trout, trembling on the edge of translucency. It doesn't replace her hands and wrists, moving through flour as sure as any trout through a stream.

During spring break of seventh grade, I helped my grand-parents at the antique market they owned in Spokane, Washington. I sat in the concession stand and took quarters for maple bars and Styrofoam cups of coffee from customers who poked through booths of dusty vintage goods: old *Life* magazines, art deco dressers, pink Depression glass, globes with three Guyanas—British, French, and Dutch. When no one was buying donuts, I wandered the booths myself. I liked the bisque and porcelain dolls that my grandmother dressed in lacy clothes. I liked anything about Shirley Temple or the Dionne Quintuplets. The naughty cocktail glasses, ashtrays, and lamps were intriguing: so many naked women turned into useful objects.

My grandmother let me choose one small thing from the antique market. What I chose was a joke of a book, the pages blank, the title in gold script on the cover: *The Art of Cooking ... And What I Know about It*, by Roberta something; the last name has since worn away. That night I wrote my first journal entry in a large loopy script no longer recogniz-able as my own. It begins with "Dear Diary" and ends on the next page with "Well, I'll fill you in on the details tomorrow. Goodbye, Allison." Somewhere I had picked up the idea that writing a diary was like penning letters to an imaginary friend.

The entry that day, April 11, 1976, was about two boys who were coming with their parents to dinner the next night. I had met them before and liked them, especially the more talkative one, Elliot; he was "really neat." But he tried too hard to sound cool, swearing and talking nonchalantly about *Playboy* magazine in an attempt, I believed, to embarrass me. Still, there was something exciting about a boy who talked like that, and, I wrote, "<u>I can't wait!</u>"

The next night, according to the diary, while my grandfather said grace at the table, Elliot and I locked eyes. I shrugged, and he laughed silently. After dinner we went downstairs with my younger brother to watch an animation of "Rikki-Tikki-Tavi," the Rudyard Kipling story. This led to a conversation about "snakes and stuff." I can still remember Elliot, a wiry, dark-haired boy who needed to move as he talked. He gestured; he got up from the armchair and squinted at something on the rug; he cracked his knuckles. His brother, light-haired Shawn, sat back against my grandmother's crocheted afghans and kept his eyes on the television screen. He laughed softly to himself while Elliot kept up a running commentary, and I tried to interject something now and again.

That night I wrote, "It's always the same thing. The boys do the talking and you go along with it and nod and laugh. I wish I wouldn't do that! But every time I'm with a boy I try to please them. I'm never myself! I'm gonna try to be different! I <u>hope</u> it works." I generalized from Elliot's behavior and ignored the fact that Shawn had said virtually nothing all evening. But Elliot was the one who interested me. And with that type of boy, I knew, my role was to nod and laugh and be something other than myself.

Already, at twelve years, I felt the awkward distance between this thing known as "girl" and this self who was me.

The Lion, the Witch, and the Watermelon

My mother, who grew up in Idaho and Eastern Washington, and my father, who grew up in Spokane, left the Pacific Northwest for graduate school and spent some years meandering, following my father's academic career: Ohio, Texas, Virgin Islands, Wisconsin. Although they found those places interesting, some homing instinct kept them thinking about the Northwest. The summer I turned twelve, my parents moved us to Seattle with no jobs and no prospects for jobs, although my mother was going back to school to become a librarian. They rented a two-bedroom house with red shag carpet and red-white-and-blue wallpaper in the dining nook. My dad found a set of metal bunk beds through an ad in the newspaper.

My brother and I had to share a room and, already bleeding, I was not happy. The only space in the room that was all mine was the top of the creaky bunk bed. I climbed up there to change clothes, and I slept with books piled around my feet.

One morning shortly after we moved in, and the reality

of sharing space with a seven-year-old Martian was settling in, I left the house to explore the neighborhood. At the end of the block was a branch of the public library, just one big room with shelves of books and some chairs, but farther than my brother was allowed to go on his own. Walking around the room, I was drawn to a paperback book on a metal rack. The cover was a black-and-white photograph of a man who looked directly at me, chin on his arm, eyes peering up. His long, pale hair caught the light, frizz glinting. Next to him, a woman looked into the distance, over my left shoulder. Her hair hung long, straight, and silky thin; her baby-doll mouth and the dimple in her chin gave her a waifish look. The square neck of her cotton sundress set off her collarbones. Below the photograph was a sentence: "In watermelon sugar the deeds were done and done again as my life is done in watermelon sugar."

I sat in an armchair in a corner of the library and stared at the cover. The author was someone named Richard Brautigan, and somehow I knew that the man in the photograph was the author. He wasn't so attractive; his hair was thinning and his bushy mustache unkempt. He had tired eyes. The woman was, though not fashion-model beautiful, compellingly earthy. They were like people I had known, younger friends of my parents and less parental, the men with long hair, the women with unshaved legs. These people moved with an unhurried grace, more relaxed than my parents. They were carpenters and painters, musicians and farmers, and I was sure they lived more romantic lives than we did. I wanted that kind of life.

I traced the bones at the woman's throat, imagined the feel of her hair, straighter and thinner than my coarse curls. She would drift through his writing mornings, moving his toast-crumbed plate to the kitchen counter, watching dust motes in the sun. Afternoons she would sit on his lap and listen to him read his morning's work. I wanted to be that kind of woman.

The sentence on the cover was the most beautiful sentence I had ever read: "In watermelon sugar the deeds were done and done again as my life is done in watermelon sugar." Three times the word "done," like a bell tolling. A life somehow lived in sweet, pink juice, distilled to its essence. I looked up at the librarians, the shelves of books, the men reading newspapers, and said the sentence under my breath, glancing back at the cover until I had it memorized.

The book as an object was itself a distillation of what I perceived to be hippie culture—and this was the mid-1970s, so the culture was waning. Hippies meant plain but beautiful women and earnest, artistic men. The black and white of the photo signaled an authentic aesthetic, simple and true. The design, with the first sentence of the novel on the cover, meant anything could happen. And the book was small and slender, like a poem in my pocket. I took the sixties home with me.

On the top of the bunk bed, I read *In Watermelon Sugar*. The voice telling the story, like adolescents everywhere, had no name and every name. "My name depends on you," he said to me. "Just call me whatever is in your mind." No Name lived in a forest, where everything was made of pine, stone, or watermelon sugar, and the lamps burned watermelon-trout oil. The people gathered for communal meals and lived a gentle life of writing or making sculptures or baking bread, but they had violence in their past. When No Name was nine, tigers had prowled the community, eating the adults. They ate his parents while he was working on his multiplication tables.

Tigers that said things like, "We're awfully sorry we had to kill your parents and eat them," were not peculiar to a twelve-year-old who loved the lion named Aslan in the Narnia series. Fantastic utopian communities were a staple of the novels I'd been reading for years. But *In Watermelon Sugar* had something new. Before thirty pages were up, No Name and his girlfriend Pauline were making love in her shack. He took off her dress and she was wearing nothing underneath. They lay down on her bed. After a while he took off his overalls.

In Watermelon Sugar was probably the first book for adults I read. Brautigan wrote in the simple sentences of a child's book: "I go to the window and look out again. The sun is shining at the long edge of a cloud. It is Tuesday and the sun is golden." The brief chapters, one only twenty-two words long, were shorter even than the chapters in *The Lion, the Witch and The Wardrobe*. But what happened in those chapters was what happens between adults.

I lay in my bunk bed, staring up at the close ceiling, and imagined myself as Pauline. She was the one in the pretty dress with nothing underneath. She was also kind, and a good cook, and a painter. I didn't imagine myself as No Name. He wandered at night, wrote when he felt like it, left one woman and easily found another. I wasn't aware, yet, of my own interest in women, so I wouldn't have recognized my sexual desires in his. But I might have wanted his freedom, his writing life, his easy walk through the nights and days of his world. Like adolescents everywhere, I ached for something inchoate, something I wanted but could not yet name. I settled for wanting to be Pauline.

Three Weeks and Four Days

These were the questions of my adolescence: What kind of woman would I be? What kind of lover would I have?

My cousin Jodi lay next to me in the bed under my grandmother's quilt. The room was one end of the unfinished attic of my grandparents' cabin, on a lake north of Spokane, and we would spend the next month of summer vacation together. The attic smelled of the wood smoke from the fire in the living room below.

I was telling Jodi about a movie I'd seen just before my thirteenth birthday in June. It's about this world in the future, I said, where you can do anything you want, have sex with anyone, take whatever drugs, but the tradeoff is that at thirty, you go into this thing called a carrousel and you float up into the air and get zapped. People think you are being reincarnated, but there's no proof. Really, people are just dying.

As our eyes adjusted to the dark, we could see the bare roof beams not far above our heads. We had spent the day swimming, and my muscles were stretched out, tired. Michael York, I went on, plays this police officer called a Sandman who catches the ones who decide they don't want to die and try to escape the domed city.

Jodi sighed. Michael York. She'd seen him in *The Three Musketeers*. He was high-cheekboned, with a sweep of golden hair across his forehead and an English accent.

There's this scene, I said, where Michael York dials up a woman for sex. He starts to kiss her, but she says no and turns away.

"But you were on the circuit," he says.

"It was a mistake." Like York, she's blonde and English. She turns out to be one of the rebels.

"Oh, is this your first time?"

She nods.

"Well, let's go have sex. Come on."

Again she says no.

This dialogue isn't directly from the movie; it's what I recorded in my diary, *The Art of Cooking*. The scene became part of a script that I wrote out in longhand on a legal tablet, based on the movie, *Logan's Run*. York, I wrote in my diary, "is soooo handsome."

Jodi was a couple of years older than I was and had become my cousin when her widowed father married my widowed aunt. Her family was stricter and more religious than mine, which made for intense conversations about whether we would have sex before marriage—she wouldn't, she said; I knew I would—and whether God existed—for her, He did; I wasn't so sure. But despite these differences, we became united in our obsession with *Logan's Run*.

The "play" I wrote took almost an hour to perform, and we performed it for ourselves over and over, in the attic, in the woods, in the garage, and on the dock in the lake. I played York's handsome Sandman to Jodi's beautiful rebel, and we would run down the dock, out of the domed city, holding hands, and leap into the lake.

As the summer went on, our games evolved. I decided I preferred the actor Dustin Hoffman, whom I had seen in *The Graduate* and *All the President's Men*, to York. Jodi and I pretended we were actresses married to our true actor loves. We wrote descriptions of our weddings and drew up blueprints of our houses. Dustin and I had a mansion in Seattle and an apartment in Manhattan. I wrote Jodi love letters, signed "Michael," and hid them in her sandals, under her pillow, in her dresser drawers. Jodi wrote love letters to me, signed "Dustin."

At the end of July, Jodi had to go back home to Spokane. I was left with my grandparents and my younger brother. My parents would be coming soon, and then we would go back to Seattle and the summer would be over. Jodi and I had prepared for this moment by writing a month's worth of notes from our lovers, each note folded into a tiny square, with the date to be read printed on the outside. Mine were in a shoebox. That night, I left my grandparents and brother downstairs by the fire, climbed the ladder, and pushed up the trapdoor to get into the attic. As usual, the attic was colder than the living room, and I hurried into my pajamas and into bed. For three weeks and four days Jodi had slept next to me. Sometimes, in the night, we had pressed our backs together. Now, it took a long time for the sheets to warm up. I thought of the shoebox of notes in the dresser, thought of turning on the light and reading every note now, instead of waiting. But I wanted to wait. My stomach ached.

That afternoon, after the car with Jodi in it had crunched across the gravel and up to the road, I had written in my diary: "I feel a strange emptiness. The bed is empty and there's no one to put my back up against. I'll probably go to bed earlier now; there's no one to talk to or dance with or write notes to."

It's tempting to read my incipient lesbianism into that story. We were girls writing each other love letters, pretending to be men. But Jodi didn't come out; she's still married to a man she met a few years later. And I wasn't in love with Jodi. I liked dancing with her, talking with her, jumping off the dock with her, pressing my back against hers in bed, but I didn't want to kiss her. If I had wanted to kiss her, I could have written a kiss into the script.

If anything, what this story tells me is how rabidly heterosexual I felt at the time. In my diary, I drew a tower with myself at the top in princess sleeves and a Juliet hat, waving my handkerchief. I wrote, "I'm here. Come get me, Prince Michael." Even though I claimed I didn't want a traditional wedding, I certainly wanted *a* wedding—and a mansion in Seattle and an apartment in New York.

But even at thirteen I knew this love affair was a fantasy. I wrote a list of what I really wanted in a boyfriend and it began with someone antiwar, not prejudiced, who liked music and wasn't a male chauvinist. He would be strong but wouldn't try to control me. He would want me to be myself. This is the bell that tolls throughout my diaries—how to find a man with whom I could be myself.

Inside Out

In my early teens, I began keeping a journal in green steno pads, which I bought at Safeway for eighty-five cents. The price stickers are still affixed to some of the pads, which have the name "Spell-Write Steno Notebook" on the cover and "a list of 500 words that are often misspelled," beginning on the front and continuing on the inside cover and the back.

The first reference to Brautigan in my journal is from January 1977, in Steno Pad #6. I made a list of the "cast of characters" in my life. Brautigan comes under the letter "B" and is defined as a "contemporary writer." Other characters include the singer Joni Mitchell, friends, cousins, and my eighth-grade French teacher. In August, Brautigan appears on a list of people I want to meet before I die. My first and only reference to *Trout Fishing in America* appears in March 1977, in Steno Pad #8.

On a clear, cold night in March, I was trying to get my twin three-year-old cousins, Sara and Warren, to go to bed so I could read the latest Brautigan book I'd checked out of the library. I got Warren into his sleeper, a flannel one-piece that zipped from ankle to neck. As I threaded Sara's little legs into her sleeper, Warren unzipped his, crowed triumphantly, and jetted out of the bedroom in his underwear. Sara's eyes went wide. She let me bend her arms into the sleeves and zip her in. I dashed down the hallway and found Warren giggling in his parents' bedroom. I picked him up, carried him back to the twins' room, and there was Sara, dancing on her sleeper. This game, a twin specialty, went on for a while, but finally they agreed to get in their beds and keep their clothes on.

I settled on the couch with *Trout Fishing in America* and my steno pad. I liked the scene of the boy heading out to fish in Portland with a string, a pin, and a piece of white bread for bait. I didn't quite understand why there was a character called Trout Fishing in America who appeared now and then, saying things like "I remember mistaking an old woman for a trout stream in Vermont, and I had to beg her pardon." But that was just the way Brautigan wrote.

About halfway through the book—his novels took only a few hours to read—I flipped open Steno Pad #8 and began to write: "I stopped [reading] 'On Paradise' Page 77, to see if a Big Bird toy could talk. It couldn't, but then I remembered another Big Bird toy just like this one. It had a string to pull that made its beak move. There was no string on this one." This was my first attempt at a Brautiganesque non sequitur. I continued to flex my mimetic writing muscles. I looked at my reflection in the window and noted that seeing myself there distracted me from the reading. Glancing around the room, I looked for more material: "There is a painting above the fireplace I never noticed before. It's like an uneven ladder I don't want to climb."

Instead of copying Brautigan's words in my journal, as I often did song lyrics, I went straight to copying his style. In my best imitation, which could win a parody contest, I wrote about pajamas:

> In preparing to put on my pajamas I often find that they're inside out. And instead of pulling the outside so it is in and I can put them on, sometimes I wonder if I could just leave them inside out but put myself in them. In other words, if the pajamas' inside is out, couldn't I, by completely covering them with my body, put them on? Then, I would be on the inside and the outside would also. It would probably be warmer.

Brautigan's books offered more than a bohemian world, where pretty women made their poet lovers paintings and wore nothing under their pretty dresses. His books gave me words and sentences, rhythms, a style. He was the first lyrical writer I'd ever read, the first writer more interested in sentences and words than story. I responded by shrugging into the pajama sleeves of his style.

And then, again, there was the sex. In one chapter of

Trout, the narrator and his wife have sex in a hot spring. She asks him to pull out early and, Brautigan writes, "My sperm came out into the water, unaccustomed to the light, and instantly it became a misty, stringy kind of thing and swirled out like a falling star." I'm thirteen, in my aunt and uncle's postwar house after my cousins have gone to sleep. I read this passage and turn back to the cover of the book, with its black-and-white photograph of Brautigan with an unidentified woman. He is wearing what looks like a felt hat, a pinstriped vest over a paisley shirt, a peacoat, and two strands of beads. She has granny glasses, a lace headband, and a cape over a skirt. They are the kind of people who have sex in hot spring pools and later write about it. They are people I could become.

My little cousins are sleeping, and I'm almost done reading *Trout Fishing in America*. I haven't closed the curtains, even as night has fallen. My aunt and uncle's house is perched on a hill in the Magnolia neighborhood, and if I were to walk to the window I would see the streetlights across the valley, shining in the cold. But instead, I look at myself in the glass and wonder whether his world is one I'll ever enter.

Fog

The first time I went to Boise was because my aunt Virginia
had been killed. My mother and I sat in silence in the backseat
behind my uncle Joe, who drove, and my aunt Barbara. We
traveled through the eerie hills of the Eastern Washington
Palouse, a desert of frost and wheat stubble. I wrote in my
steno pad:

Driving in the fog

Signs come out of nowhere

Exit 93 leads to tranquil lakes

There is a fence

Pacing the car

Making sure we don't open the white

or shave it away

Hard packed dirt becomes a background to

The lacy-frosted scrub and grass

I think of a friend singing about prisoners

And she was singing about us

My uncle had been cleaning his hunting rifles, and someone had gone to the basement and brought up an old one. Somehow the rifle discharged through the case and into my aunt's heart.

The relatives gathered in Boise. My grandparents looked, I wrote in my steno pad, like "driftwood that can't be worn down much more." I watched as the women went into Virginia's room to choose her clothes for the viewing and came out puffy eyed. A friend of Virginia's was organizing the food, the funeral, the schedule; later she would marry, and divorce, my widowed uncle. Neighbors brought casseroles. People made trips to the airport to gather cousins.

My mother had brought a handmade orange corduroy jumper for me to wear to the funeral. I sat like a lighthouse beacon among the blue and black fabrics in the family section, wishing my mother had learned her funeral protocol. When the service was over and everyone else in the church had shuffled past the body, it was the family's turn. Virginia's was the first dead body I'd seen. Without life illuminating it from within, the face was just skin over structure, an arrangement of bones.

At the cemetery, Virginia's ten-year-old daughter, Cindy, and I latched to each other, sobbing. My mother and my stoic grandfather pulled us apart: too hysterical. But hysterical felt good. On the way back to Seattle, the road again reminded me of a prison, "a freeway prison with one way out." It would be thirty-two years before I went to Boise again.

Idaho is known for millionaires, potatoes, and beautiful mountains and lakes. It's also known, as the barista reminded us, for the white supremacist group Aryan Nations. Near Hayden Lake, far north of where Arline and I would travel, the Aryan Nations had their headquarters for thirty years. As I was growing up, news appeared often in the Seattle newspapers about those Aryans in Idaho. They got in trouble for, allegedly, holding up armored cars, killing people on their hit list, and making counterfeit money. Their activities weren't limited to Idaho; in the mid-1980s, a thirty-five hour standoff on an island near Seattle resulted in the death of one of their leaders.

It wasn't until 2000, when the Aryan Nations lost a lawsuit that awarded the plaintiffs millions of dollars, that the group was forced to leave the area. Today it's a much smaller and weaker organization. Still, stickers with swastikas turn up at the Islamic Center in Boise and remaining members pass out recruitment posters on street corners.

In 1961, when Brautigan was trout fishing across Idaho with his wife and daughter, it would be more than a decade before the Aryan Nations set up shop in Hayden Lake. Not to say that the streams were running clear. Had Brautigan's face been a darker shade, crosses might have been his campfires.

In the breakfast room of the Modern Hotel, I talked back to the Fox News commentators, who were questioning the integrity of one of the men running for president. The clerk at the front desk left me waiting while she ran to her car to get a sticker: BLUE STATE GIRL IN A RED STATE. She was thirsty for people like us.

In the Boise Co-op, the cashier looked at our co-op card from Seattle and said, "It's usually us going there, the other way round." We weren't trying to mean anything with our Washington State plates and our Seattle co-op card. We were just spending a couple days in Boise before we headed into the mountains where Brautigan had done his trout fishing.

But we were wary. Arline, in particular, was afraid of the campgrounds. A hundred miles in the future, the campgrounds promised open sky and only millimeters of nylon protection against predator Aryans, the drunk, hunting kind; or the more organized, hooded kind. Arline's Spanish accent often marks her as an outsider, so she thinks about these things more than I do. I wasn't sure we were going to the Idaho of her imagination, but I was sensitive to the possibility.

In the meantime, we enjoyed Boise. Old brick-red houses with white trim reminded me of my grandmother's house in Spokane. Leafy trees hung over sidewalks. Arline had been wanting to learn about Idaho's Basque community, and we visited the Basque museum and ate chorizo at Gernika's Pub. Arline bought a beret.

Our last night in Boise we drank wine on the balcony of our room at the Modern Hotel. Across the street was Oakley Moody Service, Inc., Auto Repair. The Modern Hotel used to be a Travelodge, but it was spiffed up to emphasize its midcentury modern architecture. The owner's grandmother, a Basque woman, had owned a boarding house called the Modern Hotel in Nampa, Idaho, and it was one of the few local places that wasn't segregated; everyone was welcome. Now the new Modern Hotel's neon sign burned a cool white in the dark. We propped our feet on the railing and clinked glasses.

Back when this was a Travelodge, it would have been the kind of place my grandfather pulled into with his family in the 1950s. And if he'd had any trouble with the Plymouth, he would have poked his head into Oakley Moody Service, Inc., and asked if they had a moment to check under the hood.

Orienteering

Before we left Seattle for Boise, I had searched carefully through *Trout's* seemingly random series of vignettes for those that took place during—or were inspired by—Brautigan's trip through Idaho. To the casual reader, the book might seem a collage of fishing stories with no discernible pattern. Here the narrator watches a friend pour wine down a trout's throat. Here he fishes in a graveyard creek. But most of the fishing chapters are either from a trip to northern California or the trip to Idaho.

Of the first eleven chapters, four take place around Steelhead, California. The narrator fishes in several creeks around the Klamath River. Brautigan must have gone alone; he didn't know how to drive, and in these chapters we see the narrator hitchhiking and talking to a bus driver.

For Idaho, Brautigan and his wife bought a car, and she drove. She is quoted in John Barber's online Brautigan archives as saying that the car was a Plymouth, purchased with their 1961 tax returns. The first mention of Idaho is in the sixteenth chapter, where Brautigan, apparently long gone from the state, waxes nostalgic: "O, a long way from Idaho, a long way from Stanley Basin, Little Redfish Lake, the Big Lost River and from Lake Josephus and the Big Wood River." In eleven subsequent chapters, interspersed with prose poems about other topics, he tells stories from those places. These chapters form the book's narrative spine.

My goal for our trip was to go to the Stanley Basin and find several places: the town of Stanley, where a woman in a store calls the narrator "a Commie bastard"; Big Redfish Lake, where the narrator's wife catches minnows for the baby to play with; and Little Redfish Lake, where the narrator encounters a surgeon dissatisfied with the fishing. Little Redfish Lake is also where the family camped, and it was a particularly irresistible destination because Brautigan included the number of the actual campsite: #4. Maybe, just maybe, we would camp there.

As part of my research for the trip, I made a concordance of creeks, which I here offer for the benefit of future Brautigan scholars:

Creek	Identifier	Page(s), 1972 Dell Edition
Grider	running clear	14
Tom Martin	son-of-a-bitch	19
Graveyard	funeral-procession-on-a-hot-day	20
Hayman	almost dry	27
Owl Snuff	small	30
Carrie	sheep shit	33, 34
Paradise	a muscular thing	33, 49
Salt	coyote voices	33, 53, 54
Clear	strawberry milkshake	59
Bear	no fishing	59, 60
Valley	clouds	60
Float	good name	78

If I knew I was dying, I would want to fall in love, sing on a street corner, smoke pot, travel Europe and South America, become more confident, and meet Richard Brautigan. Not bad for the dying wishes of a thirteen-year-old who was nowhere near dying. I didn't want a car or a stereo or a pony; I wanted to experience life.

Falling in love was just a few months in my future. I started high school and fell for the teacher's assistant in my algebra class. He was a skinny sophomore with braces who worked in the school candy store. One day I bought Life Savers from him and, in algebra class, gave him one. Our hands touched. We spent the next four years together.

Several times when I was in high school, I took my guitar down to the Ave.—the main street of the University District—opened the case, and played Joni Mitchell songs for spare change. "Circle Game" was easy to play and an easy range for my alto. But my peers were listening to Queen and ABBA, and even as I sang, I was watching the eyes of people passing, expecting condescension for playing a song leftover from the hippie era.

I didn't smoke pot until college. On a spring evening, my housemates and I decorated Easter eggs, first silly ones that made us giggle, and then increasingly profound ones, which we carried silently around the house, like relics from King Tut's tomb.

I got to England in my twenties; in my forties, Arline and I went to Argentina and Chile.

Self-confidence, it turned out, would always be a work in progress.

And meet Richard Brautigan. Why him? I keep asking myself. Why, of all people, Richard Brautigan? And I keep coming back to this: It has something to do with the times I was born into; it has something to do with Generation Jones.

Generation Jones

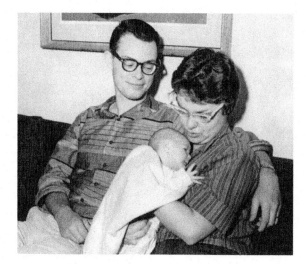

On the Road in 1963

My parents were in graduate school in Ohio when I was born. Actually, my father was in graduate school, and my mother had decided not to go back after her first year, now that she had this wiggly, complaining thing that was me. She ate a lot of cucumbers that summer I was born; maybe gas explained my wiggling.

In August, my dad waved goodbye to my mother and two-month-old me as he drove away with a friend in a '49 Ford, WASHINGTON OR BUST sign across the back. He was one of the three hundred thousand people listening to Martin Luther King, Jr. give the speech that would become the most famous in US history. According to the newspapers, there's a lot of things high school students don't know, but the "I Have a Dream" speech is one they do.

I have heard this story many, many times. I hold it like a lucky stone in my pocket, a talisman against indifference. In 1987 I went to my own March on Washington, this time with half a million people who were here, queer, and fabulous, get used to it. Marching for rights with that many people like yourself feels like Fourth of July fireworks and New Year's Eve champagne all in one holiday.

Recently, my parents told me a story I hadn't heard before: A couple of weeks after my father returned to Ohio and told my mother what had happened on the Mall in Washington, they got into the '49 Ford and drove to Alabama. They had never been to the South. My mother's sister was living in Montgomery with my uncle, who worked at the air force base.

In Birmingham, they stopped for lunch at a diner. The diner's radio was broadcasting the story of a bombing of a Baptist church right there in Birmingham, just a couple of hours before. Four black Sunday school girls had been killed. I heard about this event, which would come to epitomize the cruelty of racist Southerners, as I grew up, but I didn't realize how close I had been in space and time to the devastated church.

In the diner, my dad looked out the window at the '49 Ford with the out-of-state plates. He looked at himself and his wife and baby. Southern whites were sometimes suspicious of whites from out of state, assuming they were there to agitate for the rights of blacks. "We're not eating here," he said, and he hustled my mom out of the diner and back into the car, and they were on the road, hungry and sweating.

In Montgomery, my parents visited my aunt and uncle, who lived on the base. They had tried to live off base, but it didn't work out. Because my uncle's job was to train people from all over the world in US air force techniques, he wanted to be able to entertain them at his home. These people, from Africa and Asia and Latin America, weren't welcome in the neighborhood. So my aunt and uncle moved to a house on base. What my uncle was training them to do is another story.

At the end of September, my parents got back in the '49 Ford and drove north. According to MapQuest, they would have taken Interstate 65 most of the way. They would have driven through Alabama, Tennessee, Kentucky, and Indiana. It would have taken them about ten hours, MapQuest says, although with a baby to feed and no air conditioning, I bet it took them longer. I bet it seemed like a lifetime.

These intersections of the historic and the mundane—a racist bombing and a stop for lunch, a diaper change in Ohio and a march in Washington—are they significant? Does it matter how close I came to hearing King's words myself? Does it matter that I was born in 1963 instead of 1948? I think it does. I think it matters more than almost anything.

Girls at slumber parties have séances. Girls at slumber parties in the early 1970s had séances to raise the spirit of John F. Kennedy.

In the unfinished basement of our duplex rambler, a few girls and I sat in a circle, holding hands. A space heater blared red stripes and rumbled. We spread our sleeping bags across mattresses on the floor, and in flannel pajamas we perched on the edges of the mattresses, our stockinged feet on a frayed square of green carpet.

Who among us brought the séance lore? Not me. But we all went along, closing our eyes and holding the sweaty fingers of our neighbors. The space heater made the basement smell like singed hair. Upstairs, my mother's footsteps crossed the floor. A *thunk* was probably my brother diving into bed.

Laura whispered, "John. John." A crackle from the space heater.

"John?" Tina said, louder.

Outside, snow filled the window wells. I peeked at the hulking furnace. The fingers in my right hand twitched, and I clamped shut my eyes. It would be my fault if he didn't come.

"John!" Laura said, as if he were standing behind the furnace.

Tina breathed out, "John."

Cathy took it up, and I joined my reedy voice to theirs, opening my mouth around the syllable. We called out to him, to John, John.

What did I know of John F. Kennedy? Only that he was the handsome president, cruelly shot. The assassination was only ten years behind us, but it might as well have been in the Middle Ages for all the reality it had. There was no Internet to spread rumors, but they came through our school: Did you know Abraham Lincoln was killed in the Ford Theatre? And did you realize John F. Kennedy was riding in a Lincoln car when he was killed? And it was made by Ford? Spooky.

Our girl voices called, plaintively, for John: Come speak to us. Come tell us you're okay.

Laura was the one who opened her eyes in time to see him. Laura was always the one. She shrieked. My eyes whipped open. She pointed a trembling finger at the small, high window by the furnace. "I saw him! His eyes! He was looking in the window."

"Did you really see him?" Tina asked. The red light of the space heater flickered across her skin.

"His eyes. Those were definitely his eyes."

We looked over our shoulders. Even the puzzles and games heaped on the metal shelves looked sinister. I asked Laura if I should turn on the lights. She shrugged. "He's not coming back again." It must be my fault.

I pulled the string of the overhead bulb. We blinked. Shadows retreated behind the furnace.

Laura opened my orange-and-white plastic record player and set the arm on the 45 record she had brought. By the time the singer asked if we'd seen John, tears streamed down our cheeks. The good died young, and weren't we good?

But I think we were crying for more than our young

selves. I think we had absorbed the sadness of our parents, who held us in their arms when the man they'd felt such passion for died. And the despair they felt, five years later, when those other beacons of hope were taken from this earth forever.

Our séances didn't call forth an assassinated president; our séances called forth our parents' sorrow.

My Parents' Record Collection

My parents kept their record collection in the living room on a bookshelf made of wooden boards and concrete blocks. Some of the concrete blocks had been abandoned on a curb; my father had pulled over the Valiant and hauled them into the trunk. The shelves didn't look sad and grad-schoolish to me; my parents were a decade out of graduate school now, and all their friends had board-and-block shelving. Ours were particularly elegant because my mother had stained the boards a rich brown.

A ritual of visiting was to drop in front of the host's records and flip through the covers. Most of the records would be on the shelves, but the most recently played would be stacked on the floor facing out. Empty covers indicated what was on the turntable. Some were purists and put on only one record at a time, but others balanced several on the spindle, and they dropped in turn, thereby doubling or tripling the time until the records had to be turned over.

My parents' collection included many Beatles albums—*Rubber Soul, Sgt. Pepper, Abbey Road,* Jefferson Airplane's *Surrealistic Pillow,* and The Doors' *Strange Days.* They had a lot of classical and jazz as well, but those held little interest for me. I would lie on the couch with the *Sgt. Pepper* cover, singing along. The lyrics printed on the back cover were more magical than any children's book. As soon as that lonely voice began to sing "A Day in the Life," I was filled with a delicious melancholy that sometimes brought on actual tears.

But by the time I was listening to these albums, many of them had been out for five years or more. My friends at school weren't listening to them, and many of their parents weren't either. When I went to their houses, I didn't recognize most of the albums in their living rooms. (What must they have been—Glen Campbell? John Denver? The Allman Brothers Band?) My friends' parents, an assortment of neighbors, and my parents' friends, mostly academics, did not have the same tastes in music.

As I grew older and began reading Brautigan, my interest shifted to female singer-songwriters like Joni Mitchell and Laura Nyro. They were still producing albums, but their best work seemed, to me, to be years behind them. I was six years old when Mitchell's ethereal *Clouds* was released, and by the time I was picking out her "Chelsea Morning" on my guitar, the album was available for almost nothing in used record stores.

If I'd been born a decade earlier, I could have taken my guitar to San Francisco and played in coffeehouses. At least I could have seen Joni Mitchell perform. According to her web site, she performed twice in Seattle—in 1972, when I was eight, and in 1974. She didn't even wait for me to grow old enough to buy my own ticket and take the bus downtown.

A Pew Research Center survey found that 86 percent of Americans believe there are major generational differences over taste in music. Arline is mystified by this idea that, in the United States, generations have such distinctive tastes and identities that they can't appreciate each other's music. While it's true a new type of music emerged in Latin America from her generation, a movement of political folk music called *Nueva Canción*, and that styles of music in Latin America become more or less popular at different times, she sees the old and new cascading down through the years like streams coming together, not like separate rivers. She grew up listening to *boleros*, *sones*, *décimas*, and *bachatas*, styles that musicians continue to incorporate as they make new forms, like reggaeton (which, though associated with Puerto Rico, started in Panama).

But even at thirteen, I understood that Americans associated waves of musical styles with generations, and even slices of generations, and that I was out of step with mine. Of the bands popular among my peers, none appealed to me: the Eagles, David Bowie, the Bee Gees, Barry Manilow, Fleetwood Mac. Instead, I immersed myself in Judy Collins albums that had been issued before I was born; a friend of my parents, cleaning out, gave me his entire collection.

If I were to choose a particular year whose artistic and literary creations most impacted my life, it would have to be 1967. That year brought *Trout Fishing in America*, *Sgt. Pepper*, and my fourth birthday.

On the Lam in Newport, Washington

My favorite Beatle was George, the quiet, soulful one. I wanted to marry him, but he was already married to a waifish blonde. Later, singers like Joni Mitchell showed me that I could be a musician, not just marry one. But musicians were not the only women in popular culture to capture my attention. One woman's image was all over our black-and-white televisions in the mid-seventies. She was out there in America somewhere, and she was very dangerous.

We bought groceries in the small town of Newport when we stayed at my grandparents' cabin in Eastern Washington. The trip to Newport was an afternoon's entertainment when we felt like going somewhere. (Newport is forty-two miles north of Hayden Lake, Idaho, land of Aryans.)

One day, I exchanged my swimsuit for a sherbet-orange top and shorts sewn by my grandmother, and worked my toes into rubber thongs for a trip to Newport with my dad. We went to the paperback book exchange, where I traded

Agatha Christies, two for one. We ate lunch at the diner we always called "No Shoes, No Shrits," after the misspelling that had been posted on the door one year. While we ate our grilled cheese, we wrote funny postcards to my dad's parents.

After lunch, we went to the post office. "Wanted" signs hung on a bulletin board: scruffy-looking men who'd killed police and robbed banks. There was the woman: Patty Hearst. The picture of Patty Hearst in my head was the one at the bank where she wore a trench coat and hefted a machine gun, Patty Hearst the terrorist. But in the picture on the wanted poster, she smiled, the newspaper heiress. The news stories that tracked her movements told a strangely compelling story: culpable but not, dangerous but only if pushed. What my preteen self noticed was she was famous but not very pretty, which meant there was hope.

I said, "Patty Hearst wouldn't be in Newport. Why do they have signs for her in the Newport post office?"

My dad licked stamps and stuck them to the postcards. "Newport is exactly the kind of place Patty Hearst might be."

And maybe she was. Maybe I'd seen her buying a pound of Brach's candy at the Safeway, or paging through *And Then There Were None* at the book exchange. Must be boring on the lam sometimes.

We mailed the postcards, got into the Valiant, and drove through town. Patty Hearst was sitting in the window of No Shoes, No Shrits, drinking coffee over last week's *Newport Gazette*.

My earliest memory is from the day my mother's older brother, Howard, died. He had gone to a junkyard to find some part, and while the attendants were out to lunch, a car fell on him. I learned all of this later. What I remember is a black rotary telephone on a stand at eye level and my mother answering the phone. I crook my finger over the button that will disconnect the call and grin up at her. I'm going to push it; aren't I funny? She bursts into tears and turns away.

Some childhood memories seem tattooed into consciousness, sense impressions made in the moment. This one stayed long enough for me to ask, years later, if there might have been a moment when my mother got a call that made her cry. Maybe when I was two or so? Yes, she told me; I was two and a half when my uncle died. She remembered my response to her crying. She put me to bed, and, for once, I didn't fight it.

But other memories are based almost entirely on photographs. What I remember of a house, a front stoop, and a neighbor girl with one front tooth missing comes from the square black-and-white snapshot my father took. I can spin a whole story from that photograph, but without it, there would be no memory.

My Vietnam War memories are mediated, not only by television news reports but by songs. In fact, I have no specific memory of the war on television, and I have no memory of adults discussing it, although they must have.

Three of my uncles served in Vietnam; there must have been talk of them in the family. No one close to me died in the war; all the deaths in my family when I was young were freakish ones—my aunt killed by a stray bullet, my uncle crushed by a car, a great uncle (who worked for the power company) accidentally electrocuted on a stormy night. But no war deaths brought Vietnam home, and if my uncles had traumatizing experiences, I didn't hear about them. I had no intimate connection to the war. The television footage must have been no more significant to me than other faraway tragedies, like the people starving in Biafra.

But Vietnam became a lyric. One day I would play the songs—poems put to music by Steven Stills, John Lennon, and Joni Mitchell—on my guitar.

And it became a documentary. My visual knowledge of the war derives almost entirely from documentaries shown periodically on PBS.

The war did affect me directly in one small way. At various moments, I felt compelled to explain why my father hadn't been drafted. There was some taint associated with people who hadn't served, although I couldn't have said why at the time. I asked my dad numerous times to explain it so I could explain to my friends. First he got an exemption because he was going to college. Then he got one for being a father. My father. So I saved my dad. Not only did this story resolve any suspicions about my father's whereabouts during the war, but it also featured me as the hero. What could be more satisfying than that?

If one experience separates the early baby boomers from

third-grade class, where Mrs. Peerenboom said it would force boys and girls to use the same bathroom. And, she looked at Denise, a pudgy girl in the next desk, do you really want to work in the jungle handling snakes? That's what women's lib will do. Denise flinched. Mrs. Peerenboom retired that year.

Women's equality was debated on all my favorite television shows. On *The Brady Bunch*, Marcia insisted girls were the same as boys and talked her way into the boys-only Frontier Scouts. She passed all the tests on the camping trip—barely—but decided she'd rather read fashion magazines than build a fire. On *The Courtship of Eddie's Father*, a young feminist took the handsome widower on a date. She insisted on opening doors, tasting the wine first, and paying the check. When she wanted to stop the role reversal and pursue their romance, she got her comeuppance: Tom kissed her and lectured her on the value of "different but equal."

"Women's lib" was one of those polarizing phrases; either it sounded like freedom in your mouth or like canned spinach. The ones who spat it out must have heard liberation/landmine, liberation/liberal, and, of course, liberation/lesbian. What I heard was Marlo Thomas singing that we kids could all be free. My best friend Joanne had the *Free to Be You and Me* record, on which Mel Brooks, Diana Ross, Alan Alda, and Rosey Grier sang and told stories about how girls and boys could grow up to be anything. A pretty simple idea.

One day Joanne and I were playing a board game in her room when her mother burst into the house, followed by her friend Linda. We peeked into the living room. Winnie was furious. I had never seen such fury. In a skirt and blazer, she paced back and forth, swearing. She didn't seem to notice Joanne and me, crouching in the doorway. Linda sat on the floor, nodding, murmuring, not trying to calm her down, just listening. It took me a while to understand that Winnie had gone to a job interview for a bank manager position. When she got there, the man said, "We have the perfect job for a girl like you." Secretary. She'd gone all the way up to Menominee for that. To be treated like that.

Joanne and I slunk back into her room. I threw the dice.

But a few years later, when the woman I babysat for gave me a subscription to *Ms.* magazine, I recoiled. I wasn't one of those strident, hysterical, pushy ones. The magazines piled up on my desk, unread. When the letters asking for renewal came, I threw them away. It's hard now to understand how I could have been so fiercely feminist at some moments and so afraid of feminism at others. I must have imagined a continuum and positioned myself a good distance from what seemed unreasonable.

Reading Brautigan, around the same time *Ms.* magazines started coming in the mail, did not trigger my feminist scorn. Hippie culture was freedom loving, I thought. Life was about sharing, dancing, loving—not oppressing. It didn't occur to me that some of those hippies might have been doing more of the sharing than others; it didn't occur to me to wonder why the woman sitting on the stool next to Brautigan on the cover of *Trout Fishing in America* had no name. In any case, I would grow up to be a free woman. Because I just would.

When I was a baby, as Gail Collins reports in her book *When Everything Changed*, women couldn't get a loan, buy a house, or start a business without a man's cosignature. Before I could legally drink in a bar, the word "postfeminism" had been coined. The era between pre-and postfeminism was no wider than the kerning between two letters on this page.

Learning to Lose

The *Weekly Reader*, a children's newspaper distributed to my fourth-grade class in Green Bay, asked questions about politics, and we students voted as a class. Should a woman be president of the United States? My peers voted, overwhelmingly, "No." About that time, I took to wearing Oshkosh overalls and clodhopping boots.

Mrs. Neitzel divided the bulletin board at the back of the room. On one side, she posted anything we brought in for Nixon and for the Republican candidate for the Congressional 8th District, and on the other side, she posted anything we brought in for McGovern and for the 8th District Democrat, who was a Catholic priest named Father Cornell.

It's Danz School open house, and Mrs. Neitzel is showing my parents the bulletin board. Other fourth-graders are giving their parents tours of their desks and showing off their cursive. They are drinking juice out of Dixie cups and spilling it on the oatmeal-colored paper with solid and dotted lines where they have written their dictation. Mrs. Neitzel says to my parents that the Democratic side is a testament to my determination: I contributed every poster, flyer, and doorknob hanger on that side of the board. Mrs. Neitzel tells my parents she voted for Republican Nixon but also for Democrat Cornell, and she gives them some credit for educating her about their candidate. My parents wear the rueful grins of perpetual losers.

I didn't understand the whole Eagleton thing, when McGovern's choice for vice president was discovered to be on antipsychotic medication and kicked off the ticket. But I understood winning only one state out of forty-nine. Worse than defeat: humiliation. That was like playing no man's land and all but one of the kids on your side of the gym being hit by the ball and ejected from the game while every single kid on the other side stayed in. That Father Cornell won didn't make up for the wash of red across the map.

Father Cornell went on to win a second term but lost a third. He was running to regain the seat when the pope said priests shouldn't run for office. That was in 1980, another season of losing.

I was in high school when Reagan won, in graduate school for the first Bush. Clinton gave me hope for a few months and then approved Don't Ask, Don't Tell, the Defense of Marriage Act, and welfare reform. The election of George W. was guaranteed; the second term easy to predict. The progressives of my generation are used to losing.

In the summer of 1974, my parents kept watching the

same show on television. Men in black suits and ties sat at tables and talked and talked about something with a strange name: the word "water," the word "gate." I changed the channel, but it was the same show. Vindication didn't mean much to an eleven-year-old.

Hamburger Frying in America

We moved to Seattle in 1975, and my mother went back to school to become a librarian. My jobs were to babysit my brother in the afternoons when we came home from school and to start dinner. My signature dish was Hamburger Helper. It required browned ground beef, but usually my mother had taken the frozen chunk of meat out of the freezer in the morning and it hadn't thawed. I poured oil in the frying pan, turned the dial on the electric stove, and, when the oil shimmered, set the block of meat in it. After a few minutes, I turned the block with my wooden spoon and scraped off the part that had cooked. I turned and scraped and turned and scraped until the ice had melted and the frying pan was full of crumbled meat.

Hamburger Helper was a box and a dream. A box of macaroni and a flavor packet, and a dream of easy, delicious dinners. My grandmothers would never have made

Hamburger Helper, but it was one of my favorites. When my parents came home, we would sit at the dining table in the nook wallpapered with red-white-and-blue liberty bells and Revolutionary soldiers, and eat our Hamburger Helper and a salad made of cottage cheese, iceberg lettuce, and a canned pear.

Hamburger Helper wasn't the only thing I made with hamburger and a packet. I made tacos by browning hamburger, sprinkling in a flavor packet, and stirring in a tablespoon of tomato paste. A different packet made sloppy joes, which took sauce instead of paste and hamburger buns instead of the taco shells that came nested inside each other in a box. When my mom was in the kitchen, she sometimes improvised, to disastrous results. Canned corn in the Hamburger Helper ruined it. I was a purist. Give me meat and a packet, and I would follow the directions step by step.

We didn't always eat hamburger. Sometimes we had baked chicken, and sometimes split pea or lentil soup. If we were lucky, we had macaroni and cheese, like Hamburger Helper but without the hamburger, its packet full of a radioactive orange cheese. My brother once scarfed down his macaroni and cheese so fast that, when he threw it up, the macaronis were still intact.

Stir fries were still a few years in our future, when, in the late seventies, everyone who didn't already have a wok would buy one. My father would be the stir-fryer in our family. But for now, twelve years old, I was responsible for turning a block of ice into dinner.

On page seventeen of *Trout Fishing in America*, Brautigan describes a "Walden Pond for winos." His Walden Pond is Washington Square Park, where he drinks port wine with friends who have nowhere to go. I would not see Thoreau's Walden Pond until I was twenty-five.

We West Coast kids had a hard time in our high school history classes. The first weeks and months and even years of US history were made on the other side of the continent. Not much was going on out here, according to our history books. Some salmon fishing. Some canoe carving. Some trading in diseased blankets.

When I was in Mr. Moylan's US history class, I couldn't get my mind around dates like 1861. They might have been ten years ago or two hundred. Just like Manassas might have been three thousand miles away or thirty thousand.

When I moved to Washington, DC, just out of college, I saw Manassas for the first time. Real grass grew there— and trees. A group of young men had walked over these mounds of earth and shot at another group of men, and a lot of them had fallen right there and died. Mr. Moylan had told us that families and friends came and picnicked on the edges of the field, urging them on. (Imagine the mothers deciding what to pack. Egg salad? Too messy. Tuna? Too stinky.)

After I saw Manassas, the year 1861 started to feel like something I could touch. It was a hundred years before I was born, about fifty years before my Idaho grandfather was born. Not so far back.

When I moved to Boston, the first three chapters of the textbook started to make sense. Here was the church with the lanterns signaling Paul Revere. Here was the harbor sloshing with tea. But what I most wanted to see was Walden Pond.

I had imagined a Walden Pond that was smooth and still: water laps a pebbly shore; a crow caws from the opposite side of the pond, lifts its blue-black wings, and flies across.

What I didn't imagine was that the parking lot would fill up and I would be given a ticket to come back in three hours because only a thousand people are allowed at the pond at the same time. What I didn't imagine, dozing in Mr. Moylan's class, was how small and crowded everything would seem on the East Coast. Especially ponds. Because we have some ponds out here, and they don't have parking lots.

After Stonewall, Before Ellen

After moving to Washington, DC, in 1986, I made the deliberate choice for the first time to move into a group house occupied by lesbians. There was no Craigslist then for "rooms/ shared" with a search box for "lesbian." To find a lesbian group house in a new city—and it had to be a major city—one went to the local gay bookstore, which in Washington was called Lambda Rising, and picked up a copy of the gay newspaper, which in Washington was called the *Washington Blade* (still is). I dialed a number in one of the classified ads and was interviewed by two women who shared a house on the Virginia side of the Potomac. We liked each other well enough, and I moved into one of the upstairs rooms. Within a few days, the girlfriend of one of my roommates asked me how long I'd been out. Seven months, I told her, which was how long it had been since I first kissed a woman. She said, "You got to start somewhere."

You got to start somewhere? We say this to people who are beginning a daunting project in a small way, wearing a chicken suit for a mattress company with the hope of someday acting, or slinging fries into vats of oil with the hope of someday owning a restaurant. My big project was—what? Becoming a real lesbian? Someday I might make it if I tried hard enough? Indeed, entering "the" lesbian community in the mid-eighties sometimes felt like an effort to collect badges and fly up from being a Brownie to a Junior Girl Scout.

The first and most important badge was the coming-out narrative. The earlier you remembered preferring girls, the more authentically lesbian you were. Surely a little cousin, a girl in first grade, or a teacher had first made your knees twitch. Any relationships with men had to be dismissed as aberrations; you didn't realize yet, you were searching, you were deluded, you were in denial, you loathed yourself, you feared your desires, you wanted to please, you thought it would make you normal, you wanted to know how it felt, you were testing yourself, you were trying one last time, you were drunk. Any sparks with other girls were evidence of your true nature. Your life had folded inevitably into an origami creature, its bends and creases suddenly recognizable as something elegant.

Another badge was participating in lesbian culture. (Only later would we pluralize that word, realizing that our largely white network of urban lesbians was only one group engaged in creating community.) We listened to womyn's music, which was generally folky and sweet voiced. We read mysteries starring butch detectives who tracked down villainous men. We camped for long weekends on "womyn's land," exchanging massages and taking turns stirring pots of bean soup.

Of course, I'm exaggerating, licking the bitter wound left by the offhand comment of a roommate's girlfriend. But somehow those words epitomized our era. I'd missed the fireball that was the Stonewall rebellion and the early days of the women's movement, which had propelled large numbers of women out of the closet. Now in the mid-1980s, some of the movement's energy had burned off; narratives were congealing; the culture was growing stale.

And just as I made some peace with this culture, wedging my past into the contours of the coming-out narrative, a younger generation of lesbians emerged on the scene, and they cut the old narratives to ribbons. Lipstick lesbians, transgender lesbians, nonlesbian lesbians. Like someone named Karen, who recently posted this comment online: "I'm a queer girl, who had a trans boyfriend, and who may date (trans or non-trans) men in the future, as well as (trans or non-trans) women." She still felt awkward referring to her (trans or non-trans) boyfriend as "boyfriend."

The narrative has exploded into hyperlinks.

Meanwhile in Panama

Ten-year-old Arline and her mother huddled in their apartment, listening to the radio on what would come to be called El Día de los Mártires. Two hundred Panamanian high school students were marching to the Canal Zone with the Panamanian flag. In 1903, the United States had supported Panama in its war for independence from Colombia in order to build the canal. Panama gave the US government control of a large swath of land, the Canal Zone, which was soon populated with US military and civilians, called Zonians.

By the 1950s, many Panamanians wanted sovereignty back, and they made repeated attempts to plant their flag in the Zone. On January 9, 1964, students of the Instituto Nacionál, one of the best public high schools in the country, marched toward the Zone. They demanded that their country's flag fly over Balboa High School, which was attended by the children of the Zone. Buildings in the Canal Zone were supposed to fly both the US and Panamanian flags by then, but the Zonians wouldn't have it. When the Canal Zone governor decreed that no flags would fly in the Zone at all, Balboa High School students raised the US flag anyway.

Arline lived in an apartment a couple of miles away. She worried for the Instituto Nacionál students. What were they doing, taking on the US government on the soil it had claimed? But as the news came in, she grew outraged. The students reached the Zone and negotiated for a small group to approach the school, run the flag up the pole, and sing the Panamanian national anthem. At the high school, a couple thousand hostile Zonians gathered around. The Panamanian students were attacked, and their flag was ripped. The students ran for the administration building and tried to pull down the US flag. Police drove them out of the Zone.

Thousands of Panamanians massed at various points outside their Berlin Wall. They threw rocks and chunks of concrete chiseled from the sidewalks at the Zone police. US civilians may have fired into the crowd. A young Panamanian on his way to the movies stopped to carry the wounded to safety; he was the first shot and killed, the first martyr of that day. By evening, the US Army had taken charge.

Over the next several days, Panamanians burned cars, attacked US businesses, and repeatedly attempted to enter the Zone to plant flags. By the end of the fighting, four US soldiers and twenty-two Panamanians had been killed, including an eleven-year-old girl who had been standing on her apartment balcony and was shot by a US Army rifle.

Arline, listening to the commotion and watching smoke drift by the apartment window, burned with a feverish anger. Arline was never a flower child.

Arline was not a baby boomer, either, although she was born in the fifties. The events that led to the population jump in the US—returning soldiers, the G.I. Bill, a surging economy—didn't happen in Panama. So neither did a cultural phenomenon centered on a generation. Given US dominance and colonization, she was aware of many events that fed boomer culture—she, too, remembers where she was when Kennedy died: in her sixth-grade classroom—but she never sang along to "Abraham, Martin and John." It might be said that Arline became a baby boomer the day she disembarked the plane in Seattle, Washington, at age twenty-four.

The Idaho-Panama Connection

My mother's family was having a reunion at the lake cabin near Newport. It was the first reunion after my mother's parents had died. Her five siblings were there, and their twenty children, and their who-knows-how-many children. Arline and I had just met, and I dragged her along. My father brought his father, who didn't know anyone there but was game for the trip.

One afternoon, kids ran around with squirt guns while the men fired up the grills. My grandfather was sitting in a lawn chair, watching the activity. Arline sat next to him. "Where you from?" he asked. Everyone asks Arline where she's from.

"Panama," she said. "Where are you from?" she always asks back.

"You from Panama?" he said. "I'm from Idaho. You can stick with me."

And so the outsiders stuck together.

Out of Eden

By the end of the 1970s, the mood in the United States—at least in my United States—was bleak. Tom Wolfe said the older baby boomers, my heroes, had become obsessed with themselves and were no longer championing the greater good. President Carter was wearing sweaters and telling us to turn down the thermostat if we didn't like energy prices. And one more thing: disco.

In a cultural and adolescent funk, I took refuge in Brautigan. He inhabited an America of hope and imagination, of surreal but engrossing dreams. And what exactly was the nature of those dreams? That was one of the things I went to Idaho to find out.

Richard Brautigan Slept Here

The Scenic Route

I rescued a map from my grandfather's house after he died. On the cover, two women and a man hold hands in a mountain lake. The women wear substantial swimsuits. By "substantial" I mean they cover the hips and tops of the thighs; these swimsuits do not ride up.

The title of the map is *Idaho: Highway Map of Vacation Land*, and it was issued by the Idaho Department of Highways in 1952. Unfolded, the map has five panels. On one side are black-and-white photographs that show the kinds of vacation you can have in Idaho. Two men with rifles smile beside a dead mountain goat. A boy shows off his creel and twenty trout, arranged in two lines on the grass. Men on horses climb the Sawtooth Mountains. I don't think potato cultivation and log drives are meant to be examples of recreation, although the caption on one photograph says the "giant cedars await the builder's tools." Seems like everything in Idaho is just waiting to be shot, cut down, or gutted.

On the other side is a green topographic map with orange highways and blue lakes. The border looks like wood, as if the map was framed or tacked to a den's paneling. Months before we went to Idaho, I pinned this map above my desk. I traced the orange line from Boise to Lowman and along the south fork of the Payette, where the road stopped in 1952. Today the road continues to Stanley, and this is the road we would take there, but not before spending a considerable amount of time deliberating over whether we would camp or not.

Arline fretted about the Aryans hiding behind every tree. We both wondered about the temperature. I thought a sleeping bag and tent might be enough to keep us warm through the night, but even at nine in the morning the temperature climbed to a mere 35 degrees. So, on the drive to Idaho, we decided to camp at a lower elevation, in the Boise National Forest. While we were in Boise, we found the US Forest Service office and bought a fancy, laminated map. I unfolded it on the floor of our room in the Modern Hotel and circled campgrounds and cross-referenced them on the laptop, searching through Google images. I picked several that looked nice.

The next morning, we headed into trout-fishing country.

Emails show up periodically in my inbox with advice relevant to owning a home. Ten ways to find storage space in a small house. Eight ways to prepare a house for winter. One day it was thirteen ways to keep your house safe. Install deadbolts at least three inches long. Attach window alarms that will shriek if the glass breaks.

All this effort to keep ourselves safe in our houses, and then we drive an hour and a half, pitch a tent, and sleep with nothing between us and the scary people but a zipper.

My family didn't camp much. My first girlfriend introduced me to camping. She salivated over the gear: tent, sleeping bags, pads, tarps, candle lantern, propane lantern, coolers, flashlights, two-burner stove, nesting pots, one-cup plastic coffee filters, molded dinner plates. She even had a yellow plastic egg transporter, with room for nine eggs.

She didn't worry about camping, but I did. Too many people in a campground increased the likelihood of a bad apple hanging about; too few and the opportunities for getting away with mischief multiplied.

Sometimes she understood my fear. One weekend in early fall we drove through a nearly empty campground in New Hampshire, looking for the best spot. We turned a corner to see a dozen hunters, all men, all in camouflage, hunkered around a fire. Every eye, shadowed by a camouflage cap, followed the path of our car.

In May 1996, Julianne Williams and Laura Winans, a couple, went hiking and camping along the Appalachian Trail. They were found dead, hands bound, throats slit. Gay and lesbian newspapers across the country followed the story long after the straight newspapers had lost interest. As far as Google can tell me, the case was never solved.

As it is with stories of crime, this one looms larger than the dry statistics of the thousands, if not millions, of lesbian camping weekends that have ended in tragedies no more significant than ember-melted fleece or a lost tent stake.

Arline and I don't use our camping gear much. Getting ready for camping can take forever: finding and organizing the gear, buying more food for a weekend than we would eat all week, deciding on a campground. Then, once we're there, our dog goes crazy wild. We're living in the park! He wants to go for walks every minute. He wants to smell the other campers. While we're playing Scrabble on the picnic table under the Coleman lantern, he points his snout at the tent opening: time for bed. We let him in, and when we join him later, he's spread his ninety-four pounds across the softest part of the sleeping bags. We nudge him over and sleep fitfully, listening to him snore, but grateful for whatever protection he might provide.

Boise is a grid of docile houses and sleepy patches of grass, but strike northeast out of the city on Route 21 and the houses quickly give way to patchy scrub and a wild aridity. Hills rise, none gentle, and the highway rises over them because there's no easy route between. The houses here are the kind with shack outbuildings and old pickups panting in the shade.

The pamphlet from the US Forest Service said this road was the Ponderosa Pine Scenic Byway, and at first we didn't see what was scenic about it. But gradually more ponderosas sprang up and the air greened with their needles, and we saw the point of the occasional turnoff to look at the view.

The first campground on my list squatted next to the highway under a few spindly trees. The Google pictures had cropped out the highway. The second campground cozied up to a pretty creek, but only one other tent was pitched there. Not much protection against the Aryans when they came out at night. By the time we got to the third, we figured we were halfway to Stanley and maybe we should check it out even if the nights were cold.

At Lowman, we met the south fork of the Payette River and followed it toward Stanley. Water always puts us in a good mood. The south fork of the Payette was a vein to the sea, and seeing it running along there made us feel more at home.

The road went up and up and then leveled off, the asphalt turning dark and new. We saw no other cars. Stanley was ahead somewhere, and we were headed toward it. We tunneled through ponderosas. And then the trees gave way to range land, and the mountains thrust into the sky.

I had collected several guides to this part of the world: my grandfather's map, the *Moon Handbooks* guide to Idaho, and brochures from the Idaho Transportation Department. Of course I had *Trout Fishing in America*, in which Brautigan, who never says the obvious, said nothing about what it was like to finally see the Sawtooth Mountains. All he said was, "Driving now along Valley Creek, we saw the Sawtooth Mountains for the first time. It was clouding over and we thought it was going to rain." None of these guides prepared me for the Sawtooths. They came into view on that late summer afternoon, snowy diamonds in a blue, blue sky. They fractured the lid of the world.

We kept on toward Stanley. It turned out to be a small town surrounded by fields of sheep and cows. We drove down its main street a few blocks to a T in the road and turned left, and then we drove a few blocks to Lower Stanley. Stanley, upper and lower, is small, really small; a hundred people live in Stanley. Since we are Americans of our time, it reminded us of the town in the television show *Northern Exposure*. Brautigan writes about going into a store in Stanley where the people looked nervous. He says a woman called him a Commie bastard. I bet she didn't. I bet it's what he thought she was thinking. It's funny what hippies and lesbians have in common.

This is the trouble with camping: there's always a reason not to do it. In Stanley, we took a room in a lovely motel on the river. We could sit on a deck and watch the river glitter over rocks while sheep and cows grazed on the other side. We had a stove and a microwave oven. We had a little table to play Scrabble on. And in the morning, when frost covered our car, we could huddle in bed with our coffee and look out the window at the Sawtooth Mountains, pink in the morning light.

Brautigan's Wilderness

In one chapter of *Trout Fishing in America*, FBI agents stare at a trout stream. They look at the trees, the water, and the fish, and see a computer punch card. All through the book, humans intrude on paradise, tainting and taming it.

A fishing buddy kills a trout by pouring port wine down its throat.

Someone tries to poison coyotes with cyanide capsules.

By the end of the book, nature has been carved up to be sold at a salvage yard. Waterfalls are nineteen dollars a foot. Birds are thirty-five cents. Brautigan mourns the loss and commodification of the wilderness.

He clearly loves being in that wilderness. He—that is, the *narrator*—is constantly hitchhiking to get to creeks, bivouacking along creeks, counting the trout he pulls out of creeks. Yet he never describes the wilderness in romantic, lyrical, or sentimental terms. His descriptions are either flatly literal or slyly metaphorical, often marrying the natural world to the urban human one: a creek is narrow like a line of telephone booths, and another is like a department store.

In several chapters, Brautigan satirizes the American desire to get back to nature. One Mr. Norris, deciding to camp for the first time, buys all the gear and heads into the mountains. But the campgrounds are so busy that he doesn't get a site until someone dies and is carried out. When Brautigan—that is, the *narrator*—camps, he prefers smaller, emptier campgrounds or no campground at all. He suggests there is a wilder wilderness out there, and he wants to find it.

Glimpses of that wilder wilderness appear through the thicket of metaphors. The last time the narrator has a conversation with him, the character called Trout Fishing in America rhapsodizes about the day Lewis and Clark found the Missouri River. They caught half a dozen nice trout. Unlike the narrator, whose childhood expedition ends not at a trout stream but at a flight of stairs, Lewis and Clark were on the land when the rivers were real and the trout abundant. The narrator seems in search of that lost paradise throughout the book.

About ten years after Brautigan traveled through Idaho, and a few years after his book was published, America celebrated the first Earth Day. The US Forest Service created a character for that day: Woodsy Owl. I had a poster of

Woodsy Owl on my bedroom wall. Woodsy wore a jaunty green hat with a red feather, and green pants with a gold Forest Service belt buckle. I don't imagine Woodsy and his motto were hopeful developments to Brautigan. I imagine by the time Woodsy made his debut, Brautigan had pretty much given up on finding paradise.

A Route

I zoomed and clicked, clicked and dragged, through the gullies and ravines of Google Earth's Idaho, repeatedly consulting *Trout*, in an attempt to map what might have been the actual route Brautigan and his family took. William Hjortsberg's biography of Brautigan, with its detailed description of the trip, hadn't yet been published, so I got some of it wrong; I didn't realize, for example, that the Brautigans spent the entire summer in Idaho. Nevertheless, this was my conjecture at the time:

From Boise, they took the interstate to Mountain Home and from there Route 20 to Fairfield. They followed roads with names like Soldier Creek and Little Smoky into the Soldier Mountains. In 1961, parts of this route were unpaved. Today, parts of this route are still unpaved.

By now he and his wife and baby were several hours from

Boise, and they scoped out places to camp. Suddenly, sheep thronged the road. He drank a warm beer from the backseat. The sheep finally moved off, and they found a place to camp near Carrie Creek.

In the morning, they packed up and went back down Little Smoky Road to Soldier Creek Road to a nameless national forest road that led to Worswick Hot Springs. He and his wife spent the afternoon in the springs, the baby napping in the car. In the book, he would misspell Worswick, thinking it must have an *e* in there somewhere.

To get to Paradise Creek—perhaps that afternoon or the next day—they headed north again to Big Smoky Road. A lot of sheep were snuffling around here, too. He fished a little by himself. Who knows what his wife and baby were doing.

It was raining the next day as he fished at Salt Creek, and afterward he sat in a bar asking the guy on the next stool about the cyanide capsules for coyotes up there. Maybe the bar was in Fairfield, which is an hour or so from Salt Creek. Maybe his wife and the baby stayed at The Prairie Inn. His wife had, I hope, brought along a few books.

By now, they'd spent a week in Camas County. They headed back into Boise and drove the hundred miles north to McCall, where his wife had Mormon relatives. He bought socks. Then they drove the road to Lowman, which soon turned to dirt. Today, the road to Lowman is paved.

In 1961, the route from Lowman to Stanley went along Bear Valley Creek and through the town of Cape Horn. Today, one can drive to Stanley more quickly on Route 21. But in 1961, Route 21 petered out at the Sawtooth Lodge. In any event, Brautigan and his family reached Stanley, where he bought a candy bar and the clerk said, "You're better off dead, you Commie bastard." If that's what the clerk said.

Brautigan and his wife ate hamburgers in a restaurant while a girl played with the baby. After dinner, they headed up to Big Redfish Lake, which was mobbed with campers. They camped instead at Little Redfish Lake, site four. He was amazed no one had shot up the metal stove pipe of the grill.

They spent a few days in the vicinity of Stanley. At Big Redfish Lake, his wife caught a panful of minnows, and the baby played with them. At Little Redfish Lake, he had a conversation with an unhappy surgeon.

The next destination was Lake Josephus. At Helldiver Lake, the baby got sick. He blamed his wife for letting her sleep too long in the sun. He carried the baby down the mountain, and she revived. Leaving Lake Josephus, they ran across a monument for a fallen forest ranger.

In 1961, it was a straight shot down Route 93 from Stanley to Ketchum. Today it takes about an hour and a half, and the road is called Route 75. His wife had cramps, so he left her in a motel and took the baby to Big Wood River. On the next page, they'd gone home.

I didn't try to retrace Brautigan's steps entirely. What I wanted most was to find site number four at Little Redfish Lake. Later, I would realize I needed to see Worswick Hot Springs, too.

In a photograph online, a skinny man in jeans and a plaid flannel shirt stands knee-deep in a lake. His hair is conventionally short, not shaggy as on the cover of the book. He wears glasses and holds a fishing rod; its line bobs nearby. Behind him, on the far shore, the end of a rustic bridge is visible amid the foliage. The pictures we have of Brautigan on the Idaho trip were taken by his wife, Virginia Adler Brautigan.

Because *Trout Fishing in America* is a work of fiction, we understand the narrator's wife is a character and not really Virginia Brautigan, but we also know that the scenes in Idaho are based on the real-life trip and that the "woman who travels with" Brautigan is Virginia. So one way I grappled with this book was unearthing what I could find about her, about the woman with that name.

According to web sources, Virginia Adler was born in Idaho in 1935. She and Brautigan married in Reno in 1957 and had their daughter Ianthe three years later. Throughout their brief marriage, Virginia worked as a secretary while Brautigan wrote and did odd jobs. The summer of 1961, they spent their tax refund on a used Plymouth station wagon, loaded it with camping gear and diapers, and took off for the trip to Idaho. Brautigan fished with a bamboo rod that would be auctioned on eBay years later.

Back in San Francisco, Brautigan was moody and distant. He spent nights out with friends, leaving his wife alone with their daughter. It could have come as no surprise when she fell in love with someone else, a man named Tony Aste. She and Tony had three children. Years later, she turned up in Hawaii, where she became a community activist. She ran for the legislature in 2000.

It took me a long time to find the woman who traveled with Brautigan on the Internet. Type "Virginia Brautigan" into your browser and all you'll find is the wife of the famous writer. Today she is someone else entirely. Today she goes by "Ginny Aste," and if you type that name in, you'll find her involved with skateboard parks and community trails projects in Pahoa, Hawaii. You'll find her testifying to the Hawaii County Charter Commission on July 21, 1999, lobbying for a Department of Environmental Quality. Looks like she's the kind of woman who gets things done.

The Baby Who Travels with Him

Ianthe, never named, is the baby in *Trout Fishing in America*, the daughter Brautigan took to Idaho. She's a few years older than I am, and she has been my avatar ever since I reread his book. She grew up in the same world, more or less, that I did. She, too, is in between generations.

I doubt, when I read the book the first time, I identified

with her. She was just a baby, a prop, a device. I wanted, ideally, to be Brautigan, the writer. If that weren't possible, I would be the woman who traveled with him, his muse. And it's not that, now, I want to be his child, metaphorically as a writer or literally in some ridiculous claim to glory. Rather, I want to reach into the book and claim that baby, give her back her name, as a way to claim my own.

In one Greek myth, an Ianthe falls in love with Iphis, a woman pretending to be a man. The gods respond to Iphis's prayers and turn her into a man so she can marry Ianthe. In my adolescent dreams, perhaps the gods could have turned Brautigan into a woman, or turned women into writers, or fused writers with their muses, or whatever it would have taken for me to be able to imagine myself in the future, writer and woman, whole.

I say that I want to replace all those references to "the baby" with her name, but Ianthe Brautigan has already, of course, laid claim to herself. She's written a book about her father, *You Can't Catch Death*, and she sounds utterly grounded, thoughtful, and intelligent in those pages, as she grapples with his personal and literary legacy.

But here's what we have in common. After Brautigan and his family (that is, the *narrator* and his family) return to California, they share a cabin in the hills above San Francisco Bay. Their friends sleep in the cabin, the narrator and his wife sleep outside on the grass, and the baby sleeps in the basement. In the basement? They didn't have baby monitors then; she could have found an old razor blade and eaten it or suffocated in her sheets. Oh, those hippie parents. Mine almost had me baptized in Kool-Aid by an Episcopal priest who offered. Strange new customs were evolving.

The Object of His Affection Speaks

In the thirteenth chapter, the narrator of *Trout Fishing in America* recalls a day in 1959 when he was encouraged by a used bookstore owner to have sex with a woman who happened to come in with her boyfriend. No amount of attempted poetry—"her body was like a clear mountain river of skin and muscle flowing over rocks"—can obscure what is an adolescent fantasy dreamed in the back aisles of a bookstore. After some hesitation, the narrator, the Brautigan stand-in, looked at the boyfriend sitting complacently in his chair, took off his clothes and shoes, and "laid the girl."

Nothing like that happened.

What happened was she went into the bookstore looking for something to read, which is why people go into book-stores. This bookstore was the kind with tall shelves spaced too close together and a radiator blasting too hot and cats kneading filthy stands constructed out of two-by-fours and old pieces of carpet.

She scanned literature from *A* to *K* to *M* around a corner and ran into a young man sitting on a stool. He was sitting where Q started at the end of one shelf, R picked up on the shelf against the back wall, and S continued on the shelf opposite Q, which effectively meant she couldn't look at anything from N to Z without being followed by small pale eyes that pretended to read a book about Picasso but were moving more up and down than left to right.

He was tall and skinny, threads fraying at the hem of his long gray coat. Why was he spending so much time reading in a bookstore where the paperbacks topped out at fifty cents? Maybe the radiator was the main attraction.

She left literature and went looking in art, where the books had not yet closed ranks around the space his book had taken. The book about the photographer Gerda Taro she wanted to read wouldn't be published for thirty years, so she took down a book about Taro's lover, Robert Capa. Sunlight filtered through a dusty window as she paged through the photographs.

A flurry of cat hair preceded the man's appearance at the end of the row. The frayed coat was stained, as if he hadn't taken it off to eat breakfast, and the knees of his jeans were shiny. He had the pink, blotchy cheeks and stance of a young man who has chosen the poverty of the poet.

Her first thought was that now she could check out N to Z, but he blocked the only exit to the aisle. He slid Picasso into the slot and knelt to look at the lowest shelf. To get by, she would have to brush the hem of her jeans against his back. He tapped the spine of each book down the row, his torso pivoting toward her.

His voice was a dusty volume of the *Oxford English Dictionary* creaking open. "The Spanish Civil War."

She hadn't asked a question with that answer. She snapped the book closed.

He stood. He put his elbow on the shelf, then took it off, tucking it back into his side.

She returned the book to the shelf. Something slunk between her feet. She sneezed, and the cat looked up at her face, turned, and sashayed back through her feet.

From his back pocket, the man pulled out a paperback. She understood she was to keep it. She left the bookstore, got on her bus, and looked at the photograph on the inside flap. It was of him with a shorter haircut. She never saw him again.

But that's how she ended up in his next novel, offering her body as if it were nothing more than the copyright page.

What Was Known Then

In the chapter "Trout Fishing in America Nib," Brautigan tells a story of a man so broke he takes a job in the mountains of eastern Oregon cutting down Christmas trees. He sleeps on the cold kitchen floor of the house where the Christmas tree owners live and he "laid" a "three-hundred-pound Indian squaw." When the man and the Christmas tree owners takes the trees to Oakland and sell them, he gets paid. He spent his money on steak, a pen with a gold nib, and a "good-looking, young, Negro whore."

The chapter is not about the "squaw" and the "Negro whore." The chapter is about the pen. But the "squaw" and the "Negro whore" are those details that a writing teacher would say *show* instead of *tell* us that this man is desperate and poor. The pen is the ironic complement. Why would a man who sleeps on a cold kitchen floor and settles for the "squaw" when he wants her teenage daughters buy a pen with a gold nib? The man tells Brautigan that the pen has mystical qualities. Brautigan daydreams about a different kind of pen, a trout fishing in America pen. We are intended to chuckle first and sigh last.

But the mention of the Indian woman in the second paragraph snags the chuckle in our throats. That's what we know today. We know not to glide right through that paragraph, parasailing over the sentences. So we stop there, registering the swelling that may be the gag reflex trigger—or perhaps a virus snuggling in—and muse over what was known in 1967 when *Trout Fishing in America* was published.

A man told the story to Brautigan, is what I think. Brautigan wrote down the story. He put the story in his book *Trout Fishing in America* and copyrighted it in 1967. Donald Allen published the book for the Four Seasons Foundation. Delacorte Press published it again, and Dell published the paperback, this paperback that I have in my hands, in February 1972.

Is it fair to ask what exactly was known in 1967? What exactly could have been known by a liberal white writer in the late sixties and his, presumably, liberal white editors at several presses? And his many white readers? Maybe it doesn't matter what they could or could not have known; what they understood of the world is no more nor less important than what Others knew and understood of the world.

I like to think that if I'd been born in 1790, I would have protested the Indian Removal Act. Some white people did. I like to think I would have been an abolitionist. Some white people were. But at twelve years old, reading Brautigan, what stayed with me were not the women in the story of the Christmas tree man, but the rivers and wildflowers drawn by the trout fishing in America nib. Now the ink seeps through the pages of the book, blotting out whole paragraphs and dripping through the friendly blurbs on the back cover.

Brautigan + Misogyny = Blah, Blah, Blah

Of the relevant hits that come up when I google Brautigan and "misogyny," most acknowledge but apologize for his attitudes toward women. Jill Murphy: "Brautigan's view of women has a tad of schoolboy misogyny about it, but benignly so." Kedves: "Mild undertone of casual misogyny." Caro: "He can do no wrong (apart from the whiffs of misogyny that I can try to pretend are 'of the era')." Alex Carnevale: "Brautigan, kind of a misogynist, but we loves him so."

My favorite comment, probably because I'm a teacher, is by Molly Vogel, who seems to be blogging for a school project: "So we all know in class how Brautigan was accused of being misogynistic, egotistical, blah blah blah." She goes on to dutifully analyze his writing style.

What I think most of these bloggers mean by "misogyny" is Brautigan's tendency to treat women largely as props. The narrator's wife, who appears often in the book, never gets a name; she's just "the woman who travels with me." A woman walks into a used bookstore and suddenly agrees to have sex with the narrator in front of her boyfriend. In one disturbing passage, a fantasy spun by the used bookstore owner, a thirteen-year-old Mexican girl seduces the narrator.

All of the more egregious depictions of women come from the mouths of characters who are not the narrator. They are "colorful," these men. They are hard-living, hard-drinking, rude and crude storytellers. Maybe I could excuse Brautigan for merely reporting, without judgment, their dialogue. But that would ignore his transformation of their words as he affixed them to the page. Take the fishing buddy in "Trout Death by Port Wine." He's the one who will kill a trout by pouring wine down its throat. As he and Brautigan approach a creek, he says, "Do you know what this creek reminds me of? ... It reminds me of Evangeline's vagina, a constant dream of my childhood and promoter of my youth." He appears to be referring to the Evangeline in the poem by Longfellow. These hard-bitten storyteller types may use colorful language, but I'm guessing the exact combination of words here is Brautigan's, not anyone he ever went fishing with.

What Is Known Now

How naïve of me to want to nail this cultural artifact to a telephone pole of its time and leave it there. There are men now who would say, as casually as the man in "Room 208, Hotel Trout Fishing in America" says to the narrator, that most women have the disposition to be a prostitute. There are readers now who wouldn't glance twice at a sentence invoking the stereotype of the black pimp.

And what can one do about it? Close the book and throw it out? Burn it? Shoot BBs through it? Axe it? Take a fat, felt-tip marker and expurgate every offending line? Send scolding emails to the Brautigan LISTSERV whenever someone waxes sentimental about the first time they read him? Insert critical comments into his Wikipedia entry? Pretend he and his books never existed? Grapple?

I'm grappling.

My graduate school literature professor sits at the front of the class behind his desk, body turned toward the window, and free associates. We're reading *The Tale of Genji*. He says, "Why is it that American women don't like Asian men?" The next day his Rorschach lecturing takes him from homosexuality to pedophilia. I drop the class.

My drama professor tells us that plays about families are no good. He calls them "diaper dramas." I write one anyway. I get a B.

The director of my MFA program says that all good writers get their audience, regardless of the race, ethnicity, gender, or sexual orientation of the author. My friend is turned down by a literary agency because they already have a Korean American writer.

I write a story about a gay man donating sperm to a lesbian couple, and the professor says at least this is a story he's never read before.

Four of us students, two women and two men, form a writing group. After several outings to drink beer and talk literature, one of the men writes a story about a lesbian whose critique of a male writer destroys his life.

I stop writing until I've graduated. My muse is not in graduate school.

And Still the Girls will Read the Boys
and the Boys Won't Read the Girls

The Harry Potter phenomenon exemplifies what research has definitively shown: girls will read books with male protagonists, but boys will seldom read about girls. Boys, then, rarely have the experience of identifying with women, of transcending their gender, while girls have it all the time. Our gender is easily zipped off, excess weight, dropped away as we fly off with the (male) astronaut, pilot, lion tamer, president. Perhaps we fit a bit more comfortably in our female skins when we get to be a Nancy Drew or Harriet the Spy or whoever is this generation's female heroine, but we are game to fly with Harry on his broomstick, and when we look down at his hands on the controls, they are also ours.

Boys, though, must feel their gender is seared more closely to the bone. They can't just slide out of it. They get scaly, like snakes; they get stuck. Or perhaps imagining themselves into the body of a girl feels like taking on weight rather than losing it. Lumbering into a fat suit. The girl body is certainly weighed down with expectations. It's supposed to be still. The limbs should not flap around too much, to say nothing of the scrubbed smells and plucked hairs, the scraped and razored and plugged. Harriet was a very, very good spy; she was also quiet about it.

The woman who owned our motel in Stanley was in her early sixties, her skin young and her hair dyed. On TripAdvisor, a few people had posted comments about this woman, saying she wasn't cordial and seemed put out by having guests. She was perfectly cordial. She was also no-nonsense and would have told us if we were doing something we weren't supposed to do. Her husband came in while I was looking through a hiking book from the rack. The motel office was their living room, which had a woodstove and a view of the river, and I was trying to flip quickly through the book and get out of their living room so they could go on living in it.

But this was my opportunity to ask what the cows and sheep did in the winter. I was still amazed that in early September the temperature at nine in the morning was around freezing. The husband, who wore a cap and a smile, said the cows and sheep are carted down the mountain every year. A migration in trailers. These particular cows and sheep, he said, belonged to the people in the ranch down there, and he pointed at a sprawling compound at the end of the valley. They were Mormons, and every year they had a big party. Even the non-Mormons like himself and his wife went and had a lot of fun. He had his own ranch a few miles beyond, but he and the motel owner had recently married, and he went back and forth between the house on the river and his ranch. He kissed her, and she smiled at his smiling face under the cap. The myth of the taciturn rancher broke right there.

Meanwhile, I was trying to sort through all the hiking possibilities. "Why don't you just take the book to your room?" the woman said. "I'm not going to need it." I thanked her, and she said, "You girls have a good time," which might have been code that she knew Arline and I weren't college roommates who'd found each other on Facebook and decided to take a trip together. "You girls" just sounded like "you girls who are a couple," not "you girls who are friends." Lesbians tend to listen for these nuances.

I walked into the sun of late afternoon, went around the next building, and climbed the stairs to our room. If these cows and sheep couldn't sleep through a Stanley winter night in a barn, then it wasn't surprising that I couldn't sleep through a Stanley late-summer night in a tent. And so I justified my own tenderness.

Trucha Frying in Panama

Arline and I had been together two years when she took me to Panama. It was a bring-the-girlfriend-home-to-meet-the-family visit. Arline's sister, Manena, and her husband, Andre, picked us up at the airport, and we stayed in the city in their fancy high-rise apartment. I met friends and family and saw the sites: the Canal, the ruins of the first

Spanish settlement on the Pacific coast, the apartment in which Arline grew up. Everyone was kind and seemingly approved of me. But after a week, we needed time alone. Manena and Andre had honeymooned near Cerro Punta in the countryside, and they recommended a place called Cabañas Fistonich, owned by a Panamanian and her Croatian husband.

We drove hours from Panama City to get to the province of Chiriquí, and as we climbed into the misty green mountains, we began to see poinsettias the size of houses. Small farms grew vegetables, coffee, and—the specialty of the area—strawberries. We passed a chalet that sold milkshakes of fresh strawberries and cream.

Our cabaña was delightful, if not glamorous. It was nestled with a few other cabins in a small valley by a river. What to eat for dinner? We had a bottle of wine we'd brought from the city. A roadside stand sold us broccoli, young potatoes, and leeks. Nearby was a rainbow trout farm, Truchas de Bambito. The guidebook talked about it; Manena talked about it. We would go fish for our own trout.

When I think farm, I think of cows munching grass in a pastoral paradise. But fenced areas of the ocean and buildings of cages are also farms. At Truchas de Bambito, the trout grew in rectangular concrete pools, and we walked along the paths between them, looking down at the baby trout, the adolescent trout, and the grown-up trout of the size we were about to eat. We felt silly renting a fishing pole, so instead we watched the attendant pull a trout from a holding tank. He took it away to be cleaned.

Americans of the Northern kind have something to do with why there is a rainbow trout farm in Panama. Immigrants from the north came to the beautiful mountains of Chiriquí and looked in the beautiful rivers and said, "All that's missing is the rainbow trout." So they had some shipped in, and they threw them in the river, and the rainbow trout, with no predators and lots to eat, proceeded to multiply and multiply and crowd out the local fish, and today they are everywhere, including a concrete trout farm outside the Hotel Bambito.

We took our trout back to the Cabañas Fistonich, where the sun was slanting low across the mountains and the river was running high and brisk. I channeled my grandmother in the tiny kitchen, pouring oil into the warped pan and waiting until it slicked across the uneven surface. I set the trout in the pan, and the oil spit and whistled. Arline poured me a glass of wine. The cramped space gave us the excuse we didn't need to stand close.

I removed the lid just as the trout turned from translucent to opaque, and we sat on the front porch, sunglassed eyes gazing into the sunset, drinking wine and eating the trout that had braved the trek from the small, concrete pool of the minnows to the big grown up pool. Its flesh was firm and tasteless.

Shivering

Arline and I woke up in our Stanley motel room and peeked through the curtain at the Sawtooth Mountains. They were very close, pink and jagged in the dawn. Below the window, frost coated our car. We'd spent the previous afternoon drinking wine on the deck by the river, and it was stunning to see how low the temperature had dropped overnight. "Who's going down to the car to get the coffee filters?" Arline asked. I looked at her. She looked at me. This excursion had been my idea. I pulled on sweatpants, jacket, socks, and shoes, and still was unprepared for the slap of icy air as I opened the door and ran down the stairs. I got into the plastic bin in the trunk and dug through the camping gear for the mesh filters and the beans we'd ground before leaving Seattle. Back in the motel room, I rubbed warmth into my cheeks while Arline got the water boiling. Although the sun was out, it would be several hours before the temperature felt like summer again, so we took our time eating breakfast and played a game of Scrabble.

Finally around noon we could leave the motel without freezing, and we headed toward Big Redfish Lake, a few miles outside of Stanley. Brautigan describes an afternoon here, where the preoccupation of the day is trying to catch some of the dozens of minnows that swim in the shallow waters near shore. A University of Montana engineering student tries a modified coffee can. Children reach into the water with their hands, but the minnows slip through. His wife puts a pan coated with leftover pudding in the water and lifts up a panful of minnows. She puts the pan on the shore, and the baby plays with the little fish.

We parked in the lot at Redfish Lake Lodge and walked to the shore. Big Redfish Lake was a beautiful high-altitude lake ringed with piney trees. The sand beach in front of the lodge looked artificial; most of the shore was rock and scrub. No one was boating or swimming—too cold. But people were coming and going from the lodge, and we wondered if we should move here for the night. Brautigan doesn't mention the lodge, but it was built in 1929 and must have looked similar in the 1960s to what it looks like today. Inside, it had a log-cabin coziness, and we asked to see a room. The teenage clerk gave us a key to the only room left and directions to find it. We went out through the back of the lodge and found a recently built cabin on the parking lot. The room might have been in a Days Inn or Best Western. The view was parked cars. We returned the key.

Back outside, we walked on the dock. Although no people were on the beach—no engineering student, no children, no mother with a leftover pudding pan—the minnows were still there. Dozens, hundreds. Tiny silver fish like coins, like wiggly paperclips. I crouched on the dock, delighted to see them. The minnows were still there.

Near the lodge was the campground where Brautigan's narrator and his wife first look for a camping spot. The campground is too crowded; Brautigan compares it to a skid row hotel. Arline and I walked over to Glacier View Campground, where sixty-three sites sprawled in all directions, and it wasn't hard to imagine it at the height of the season, chock-ablock with tents and trailers, children shrieking, mothers chiding, fathers growling, a haze of fire smoke. We could imagine Brautigan and his wife shaking their heads as she nosed the Plymouth between bikes and dogs. They looped through the campground and headed for Little Redfish Lake instead.

In the chapter "The Teddy Roosevelt Chingader'," Brautigan describes the picnic table in campsite #4 at Little Redfish Lake. He (that is, the *narrator*) notices that the metal pipe on the stove—it must have been one of those chunky old stone-and-steel ones that used to squat in campsites—has no bullet holes in it. He marvels that this campground is so much quieter and less crowded than the campground on Big Redfish Lake, and he wonders if a plague has swept through. He is happy to be here with a site right on the lake and a beautiful mountain view.

Based in this campsite, the family explores the area, and from these adventures Brautigan wrote the chapters that comprise the heart of the book. According to Hjortsberg, the writer and his family camped here for a month. Most significant is the chapter about a surgeon fishing in Little Redfish Lake. He kills a chub salmon for no reason except to demonstrate to the narrator the sharpness of his knife. He complains about his job, about fishing, about Idaho. He seems to have every advantage, yet nothing is good enough for him. They part ways at the end of the chapter, and Brautigan writes, "We were leaving in the afternoon for Lake Josephus, located at the edge of the Idaho Wilderness, and he was leaving for America, often only a place in the mind." I love this line. Both men are leaving, but one is going to a real place while the other is going someplace that doesn't exist outside his unhappy mind. The surgeon's journey ends the chapter on a melancholy note. Despite the shimmering beauty of the lake, the surgeon cannot and will not be content.

The sadness evoked by this chapter is a note struck throughout the book. Again and again Brautigan contrasts the beauty of nature with materialistic human society. He skewers self-absorbed Americans and their inability to appreciate the wilderness. The narrator escapes briefly to the forests and lakes but is inevitably forced to go back to the city.

I was not expecting to see the same picnic table or the same stove at campsite #4, but I was expecting to be able to tell which campground Brautigan was referring to. It turned out there are two campgrounds on Little Redfish Lake: Chinook and Mountain View. Brautigan didn't say there were two campgrounds; maybe there weren't two then. We found site #4 of Chinook Campground, but it didn't have a great view of the mountains, not like the one Brautigan described. So we drove into Mountain View Campground and found site #4 there. This site, not surprisingly, had a perfect view of the mountains.

Now I stood in the campsite where Brautigan and his wife and child had spent the month of July in 1961. A yellow tent was pitched next to the picnic table, but the campers and their car were gone. Beyond the table, Little Redfish Lake glittered and the Sawtooth Mountains rose into clear blue sky. Arline stood next to me as I cracked the book's already broken spine. I read aloud:

> Unit 4 had a big wooden table with benches attached to it like a pair of those old Benjamin Franklin glasses, the ones with those funny square lenses. I sat down on the left lens, facing the Sawtooth Mountains. Like astigmatism, I made myself at home.

Waves slipped onto shore and slipped back. A bird took a dirt bath in a dried puddle. Arline and I listened as my words rippled into the near silence.

Thirty-odd years after reading *Trout Fishing in America* and living in the world Brautigan had created on the page, I'd found the place in the world where the real man had pitched his tent. I could see Brautigan sitting at the picnic table, composing the chapter about the unhappy surgeon on the typewriter he'd brought on the trip. I saw him write that line about America, "often only a place in the mind." And it occurred to me that while I had spent my adolescence wishing I'd been born ten years earlier, old enough to be a hippie, Brautigan had wished he hadn't missed an earlier, more pristine American wilderness. We both ached for a lost Eden, but in the end, he sat down at the picnic table and tried to make sense of the world he'd inherited: sparkling rivers, lively trout, materialistic Americans, a commodified paradise. He turned his contradictory experiences into poetry, into *Trout Fishing in America*. I'd followed the book all this way, into the heart of Idaho, to find that Brautigan's paradise was not a place but an action: the making of art out of confusion.

Although there was a tent in the campsite, much of the campground was empty. It wasn't empty because of some Armageddon that had eliminated the people from Stanley Basin—it was empty because school had started, and the nights are cold in that area in September. But it was hard not to think that something had happened in the forty-seven years since Brautigan's visit, something had driven them away, and now the lakes were by themselves with their mountains and minnows. Maybe Brautigan's plague had swept through after all. I felt like a pilgrim to an abandoned religious site.

Tap-tap-tap

Near Shawsville, Maryland, where the Black Horse Tavern once stood, a sign says GEORGE WASHINGTON STAYED HERE. All over Europe, toes and fingers of the saintly ones sleep in glass cases, proof of their living. What is the Shroud of Turin if not proof that Jesus slept somewhere on this earth? I'm going to start a campaign to erect a green forest-service sign at campsite #4 in Mountain View Campground that says RICHARD BRAUTIGAN SLEPT HERE. I want the campers to know whose ghostly typewriter they're hearing.

Ancestors

Back in the Day

My girlfriend-at-the-time and I were driving west on Interstate 94 through Montana while I read my maternal grandfather's memoir aloud. My grandfather grew up in the Miles City area, and when we got to Miles City we drove into town and took pictures of his high school, which was a squat brick building much like my high school in Seattle. In the Miles City cemetery we found the headstones marking the graves of his parents.

My grandfather grew up on a farm, and in his memoir he talked about going to Moon Creek School as a child. Not long after we left Miles City, there was a sign for a Moon

Creek. I shouted and my girlfriend-at-the-time took the exit and we drove into a gray, rolling land with nothing on it. We found a Moon Creek School, too new to be the one my grandfather had attended, but I took a picture of the peeling black letters that spelled out its name on the mailbox.

Back on the interstate, I continued to read the memoir. My grandfather went to high school and then to what was then called the Agricultural and Engineering College, now Montana State University, in Bozeman. The summer of 1929 he married my grandmother. *Wait a minute*, I thought. I read the date of the wedding and I read the date of my aunt Barbara's birth and I was shouting again. Five months. Five months from wedding to birth. It had been six months from my parents' wedding to my birth. No wonder, when my mother told her mother about the pregnancy, my grandmother said, "Well, we'll have to make sure you have a wedding dress that fits." You know that myth that back in the day people didn't have sex before marriage? Right.

My grandfather's parents had come to the Moon Creek area to farm. My great-grandfather had worked as a brakeman on the Northern Pacific Railroad in North Dakota and had been lured by railroad and government propaganda to homestead in Montana. But this wasn't farmland. It was dry and dusty, hot in summer, frigid in winter. Grasshoppers ate the heads off the wheat. Russian thistle invaded the cornfields. My grandfather went to college to study agronomy so he could help the farmers. He later became a soil scientist for the State of Washington.

And what happened was his fifth child had the luxury of going to college to study literature, and her daughter went to college to learn to write it, and in four generations a family went from planting seeds to reaping words. So shall you sow.

Tucked In

I've seen a baby born, seen the hair-plastered head crown and the mother bear down and the whole head emerge, slick limbs and body slipping into the midwife's hands. I telescope myself back to infancy and slip feet-first back into my mother. She shrinks to her smallest self and into my grandmother. We're Russian nesting dolls, and I'm still the littlest one, still the one deepest inside.

I was born during a time when doctors knocked women out during labor. My mother says she'd been given a shot and felt drunk. She started yelling, and a nurse put a mask pumping ether to her face. When she woke up in the operating room, a nurse was cleaning up, and the baby was gone. She asked, "What did I have?" The nurse looked at her wristband and gave her the news. By the time she saw me, I'd been washed and swaddled. She never saw the doctor.

This story didn't faze me until I attended a birth and tried to imagine my mother's body lurching through labor without her. Ether was worse than restraining a woman's arms and legs, which was also done back then. Worse than berating a woman for making noise. The doctors took my mother's conscious self out of the process so they could grab the baby's head with their hairy hands without having to hear one inconvenient word from the organism who happened to be the mother. And I'm sure they assumed it was in her best interest.

My grandmother probably got the same treatment. The night my mother was born was a warm August Sunday. When my grandparents got to the hospital in Pendleton, Oregon, my grandfather rattled the doors. They were locked. Someone ran to wake up the doctor. But my mother was my grandmother's fifth child, so she was good at it by then. I bet she wasn't one whit afraid, and my mother came so fast maybe the doctors didn't have time to knock her out. I bet she didn't dawdle afterwards in the hospital either. My grandmother was not a dawdler.

Over the years, my grandmother would get up early to bake pies for a diner, sell fabrics and thread in a sewing shop, braid rugs out of wool coats bought at Goodwill, sew her grandchildren shirts and shorts and dresses, embroider pillows, paint apples and pears on pieces of wood my grandfather sanded, make lacy clothes for her collection of antique dolls, and sell collectibles in a flea market she owned with my grandfather. She didn't like seeing us sitting idle. We'd be lying around in our swimsuits at the lake, and she'd say, "If you're not doing anything else, why don't you husk that corn?" Or she'd get out bits of fabric and start us on a project sewing doll clothes. Afternoons three or four of us cousins, even my clumsy little brother, would be sitting around the living room, embroidering or crocheting or cross-stitching.

Just thinking about those days makes me feel tucked inside my mother, inside my grandmother, in a blanket of flannel and wool.

Road Trips in My Blood

If it matters to this story that I was born in 1963, then it matters to whom I was born. A mother who studied literature, a father who studied anthropology. And they were born to men and women making their way in a sometimes-harsh western United States in sometimes-harsh times.

In 1928, my paternal grandfather drove a Ford Model T with a friend from Grangeville, Idaho, to Michigan, where his sister lived, and then took the train to New York. He spent a year at the American Radio Institute learning about radio. One day he was walking down a hallway at the Radio Corporation of America, and someone motioned to him to come into a studio. In the control room was a camera, and outside the booth was a man smoking. On the camera screen my grandfather could see the smoke wafting from the cigarette. Television was born.

The 1929 Crash came, and he couldn't stay in school. He became a telegraph operator on a freighter that went to the Dutch West Indies. On his forearm he got a telegrapher's tattoo, a magnet and lightning bolt. My grandmother, whom he would marry some years later, disapproved of tattoos, and he would wear only long-sleeved shirts for the rest of his life.

Back in the Northwest, my grandfather went to school at Washington State College, as it was called then, and studied engineering. He didn't graduate, but he found a job with a television station and bought a yellow roadster. It was the yellow roadster that first caught the eye of my grandmother. She was living in the same boarding house in Spokane as my grandfather, and working as a secretary in the tax assessor's office.

My grandfather had a photograph album documenting his road trip from Idaho to Michigan in 1928, and I've been fascinated by the story ever since I first heard it as a child. I got used to long road trips early on. Every summer during the five years our family lived in Green Bay, we drove to the Northwest and back. I learned how to amuse myself in the backseat, staying cool with a bag of ice when the sun beat through the open window. My mother gave my brother and me each a shoebox with wrapped presents that we were allowed to open at intervals: a book, a pack of cards, word puzzles. Dad sometimes smoked a cigar, and the sweet smoke drifted through the car.

I can't imagine what it must have been like to drive a clattery old Model T across the country. But what that story told me was that traveling was in my blood. As an adult,

I've taken several cross-country trips, and I've noticed that when I drive a long way and finally arrive at my destination, something in me wants to get back in the car the next day and keep driving. It's hard to stop the wheels once they're turning.

The Celebrities of Cambridge Cemetery

Until I journeyed through Boise to the Sawtooth Mountains, the Idaho I had seen was a place of funerals and graveyards.

In 1995, my brother and I drove from Seattle to Cambridge, Idaho, to see my paternal grandmother's grave. She had died the year before. My parents and my grandfather came down from the lake cabin near Newport, and my aunt and uncle drove up from Sacramento. I'd never been to Cambridge, so I was concerned when the only instructions we were given was to meet at Bucky's Diner on a particular afternoon. How would I find this Bucky's? None of us had cell phones then.

My brother and I laughed when we drove into Cambridge and found that Bucky's Diner had one of the tallest signs on the only main street in town. We pushed through the glass doors, and my aunt and uncle waved from a booth by the window.

Later we paid our respects in the cemetery. A marble slab lay flat over my grandmother's grave, her dates of birth and death engraved on one side. The other side was smooth, unmarked. I wondered how it felt for my grandfather to see the place where his name would go. It wouldn't be there for another decade.

My grandfather had decided to bring his wife's body back to Cambridge, the town where she was born and left as soon as possible. I imagined her thoughts: *Goodbye and good riddance! I'm no ranch wife, no kitchen gardener.* She went to secretarial school and made a living with her hands on a typewriter. In Spokane, she met the man with the yellow roadster and convinced him to move to the more cosmopolitan west side of the state, where she grew roses and, like other white, middle-class strivers of her time, became a Japanophile and joined the Ikebana club. She took her granddaughter to the Seattle opera.

After we spent some time at my grandmother's grave, my uncle introduced us to the Tuttles. They had eight little headstones in a row; six Tuttles had died in the span of a week. Bryan, 18, died on a January Sunday in 1922. His sisters Harriet and Hazel succumbed the next day. Brother Edmund went on Tuesday and Randall on Wednesday. Father Charles passed on Thursday. Their mother Harriet Ann, thanks to God, had already died in 1920 and didn't live to see the tragedy.

Was it Hazel who hadn't learned her mother's canning lesson? Or the patriarch, Charles, who should have seen the spinach blooming in the cans? Was it the specter of botulism that set my grandmother, then nine years old, to dreaming of the outbound road? Mary Loretta Warren Green, born January 13, 1913, Cambridge, Idaho, died April 14, 1994, Seattle, Washington.

The Mysterious Beyond

For me, Idaho is both an ancestral and literary homeland. I probably wouldn't have taken a road trip to Brautigan's Idaho if I hadn't also wanted to see more of my own. But because my earlier experiences with Idaho had been mediated by death—my aunt's funeral, the visit to my grandmother's grave—I couldn't help but see the whole state as a kind of historical landscape. I kept thinking that my grandfather must have driven these roads, that my grandmother must have known people who lived in this town. Stories told at family dinners came to mind: my great-grandfather had had a mining claim and my grandfather and his brothers had endlessly and fruitlessly searched it for silver; his mining cabin had been dynamited by people who didn't like his temperance campaign. Notwithstanding the many Idahoans living out their daily lives in the present, I was driving on a highway of an earlier time.

Once more Cambridge, Idaho, is called upon to part with one of her old-timers and most respected citizens. Mrs. M. V. N. Hall, wife of George Hall, passed to the mysterious beyond on Saturday, July 21, 1917, at 1:45 p.m. and was buried in the Cambridge cemetery the following Monday. [...] A faithful wife, a patient mother, a true friend and a good neighbor, she held the respect of all who knew her.

My father once gave me a photocopy of this newspaper obituary with a hand-drawn chart. The chart showed my brother and me at the bottom, branches spreading up through my father, grandmother, and great-grandmother to Mrs. M. V. N. Hall, that is, Mary Norley Hall, my great-great.

According to the obituary, Mary Norley was born in 1849 in Des Moines, Iowa, went to Oskaloosa College, and taught school for ten years. At twenty-four she married George W. Hall and they moved to Springville, Utah, where she became a Mormon. At the age of fifty-two, she and George moved to a ranch in Cambridge.

The obituary says she had seven children, although my father listed only five: Lora Lois, Ruby Jane, Newt, Charlie, and Enid Grey. Enid, I know, ended up in an institution, rocking her life away. Ruby became a practitioner of Christian Science. Lora is my great-grandmother.

Why do we care so much about our ancestors? We can't know them. We can't truly understand what it meant to be them, to live in their time. I inherited a beautiful oak dresser from my great-grandmother, Lora Lois Hall, and when I look in its oval mirror, I try to see through my hazel eyes into hers. She must have been tough, an Idaho ranch girl, but the woman in the wedding portrait looks soft. So she is tough and soft, capable and gentle. But the woman I conjure is entirely of my imagination. I invent my ancestry. My biological forebears are no more known to me than my literary ancestors, like Brautigan, but no less real either.

Influence and Anxiety

In a café on Newbury Street in Boston, I cracked open a book on revision for creative writers. First term, Master of Fine Arts program, 1988.

The introduction went on at length about Harold Bloom's famous theory from *The Anxiety of Influence*: the poet is Oedipus, who must kill his father/predecessor poet in order to create something original himself. Mystified, I drank my coffee and looked out through the dusty windows at my first New England autumn. My influences were not overbearing fathers. They were more like older cousins who'd had the courage to travel to places we could not picture (there being no Google Earth then) and send back postcards. Doris Lessing sent dispatches from Rhodesia, where she tried to fight the good fight and find love, too. Virginia Woolf rowed to the lighthouse and flashed back beacons of warning and hope. Richard Brautigan signed his postcards "Trout Fishing in America," but I knew they were from him.

Many feminist critics have countered Bloom. If the male writer is Oedipus, for example, the female is Demeter or Antigone. But that afternoon on Newbury Street, I wasn't thinking about Bloom's sexism; I wasn't scrolling through what I knew of Greek myths for a better one to write myself into. Rather, I worried: if I saw my influences as friendly older cousins, then maybe I wasn't combative enough to forge something new out of words. Maybe I needed to argue with my influences more, refuse their postcards, write over the top of them.

Several semesters in the future, in my independent study on feminist literary theory, I would develop a righteous critique of Bloom. But today his ideas just make me laugh. Artist as Lone Genius. Poetry as a Straight Line through the Ages. Poet as Dog Pissing on Trees. (My dog will engage in a pissing competition long after he has any piss to spray.) I'm back to thinking of my influences as cousins: older, braver, more sophisticated members of my family who have always taken a kind interest in my welfare. I didn't choose them— family isn't chosen—but they are the family that my circumstances gave me.

As a graduate student, I was so many years past my first experiences reading Brautigan that I didn't think to apply my new feminist analysis to his books, whereas reading *Trout* before our trip to Idaho, the sexism and racism were almost all I could see. But part of grappling means understanding what drew me to his work in the first place. We're all awash in the prejudices of this world; it's no surprise that they appear in our writing. They appear in my own.

So I take out Brautigan's postcards yet again. And this time I focus on remembering how wonderful it felt to get them.

My Inner Trout

Keith Abbott, in *Downstream from Trout Fishing in America,* describes Brautigan's style as consisting of deceptively plain sentences that provide comic contrast for his outrageous and surrealistic metaphors. Here's an example: "We decided that we were too young to camp at Big Redfish Lake, and besides they charged fifty cents a day, three dollars a week like a skidrow hotel, and there were just too many people there. There were too many trailers and campers parked in the halls. We couldn't get to the elevator because there was a family from New York parked there in a ten-room trailer." The pedestrian "besides" and repeated "there were ... there were ... there was" give way to a metaphor that grows more amusing as the sentences continue.

Because Brautigan is more interested in his sentences and paragraphs than in conventional narrative drama, his novels are not dramatic. Abbott argues that the style is the drama, any resolution achieved by metaphor. All these years that I've struggled to write I have had the same problem. I'm more interested in sentences and paragraphs than in narrative momentum. Recently I reread my first published story and was surprised at its unapologetic lyricism: "Twenty years ago, under cover of streetlights, Gavin sashayed across this street in his mother's wig, mascara and mink. The asphalt was smooth and black. Now my sandals sink in gray depressions, and a pink-stained popsicle stick sticks to my sole." I took that story and stretched it into a novel, adding a third major character for drama. But I was still more interested in the images that knit the scenes together than in the scenes themselves. In the years since this novel was published, I have sometimes reread the opening prologue, enjoying the sound of its words in my mouth. But I have also found fault with myself for not developing the plot sufficiently, for not digging deeper into the characters. In subsequent projects I have pushed myself to expand scenes and to write longer manuscripts—to make a more conventional novel. None of these manuscripts has satisfied me, and none of them has satisfied an editor.

Now I see that perhaps I did not want to—or could not—write conventional novels after all. My desire to write poetic prose kept trumping my desire to tell a story. When, after three novel ideas failed to come to fruition, and I threw the drafts in a drawer and took my copy of *Trout* to Idaho, maybe the trip was my imagination's way of returning to the source of inspiration for all my writing.

Can metaphor and style make for resolution? I say they can. *Trout Fishing in America* was one of the most satisfying books I ever read. Those deadpan sentences with their flights of metaphorical fancy lifted me right out of my life.

In September 1984, Brautigan shot himself. If I heard about it, I didn't write it in my journal—that was the quarter I was taking a novel class in college and writing twenty pages a week. In a couple of years I would give away all of my Brautigan books except *Trout*. But now, as I read and reread the book, I still find sentences so resonant it's as if they have been living inside me since I first read them.

What the Scholars Tell Us

One scholar, from the 1970s, says the theme of *Trout* is escape into the imagination, now that escape into the wilderness is no longer possible. Another says it's that the real America is far from the ideal America of our imaginations. A third, from the 1980s, says it's the triumph of art over death.

While these critics placed Brautigan firmly in the traditional American canon, others called him a minor, regional author with limited appeal. And by the 1990s few critics were writing about him at all. His later books were not as well received as his earlier ones, and once he died, no more books were forthcoming. *Trout Fishing in America* was rereleased, however, in 2010 with an introduction by Billy Collins, and William Hjortsberg published a doorstop of a biography in 2012. His star began to rise again.

But all this talk of literary timelessness, of entry into the canon, of art beyond death, makes me think of the library in Brautigan's novel *The Abortion*. Anyone can drop off a manuscript at this library, and the librarian will catalog it. Artless or artful, each manuscript gets its shelf. Ursula K. LeGuin imagines a similar library in her novel *Always Coming Home*, but in hers, when the shelves fill up, some books are removed and destroyed to make way for the new. When I first read this book, I was shocked that LeGuin could seemingly condone such a system. In the world of *Always Coming Home*, LeGuin's own work, wonderful as it is, would one day be destroyed along with volumes of saccharine poetry. But gradually the idea grew on me. New writers are always coming up; why not make room for them? The canon is never only about quality but also about who has the power to decide. In any case, even if everyone could agree on what makes great literature, none of us would have the time to read it all.

And so did Brautigan's books have their days on the shelves, and so did the works of his critics. And some of us read and loved his books. And some of us reconsidered and grappled with them. However, art does not triumph over death, regardless of what *Trout* suggests. Let me tell you: even *Moby Dick* will not survive forever. Long before the earth falls into the sun 7.6 billion years from now, some librarian will come along and sweep it off the shelf.

A Girl from Idaho

On cool summer mornings I would sit on a stool in my paternal grandmother's kitchen and eat stewed plums while she made me pancake rabbits. In the afternoons, she played nursery rhymes on a baby grand piano, and my grandfather recorded me on his reel-to-reel singing along. When I was a teenager, my grandmother took me to the opera, and for my high school graduation we went to a season of plays: *The School for Wives*, *Antigone*, and *The Rose Tattoo*.

The Idaho farm girl had been eclipsed by the Seattle opera guild and Ikebana club president. She and my grandfather traveled to Europe, Mexico, and Japan. She collected dozens of silver bracelets, and they jangled against each other, up and down her arms.

It used to be that when Arline said I was from Idaho, she wanted me to acknowledge my Idaho heritage, by which she meant not the baby grand piano and *The Tales of Hoffmann*, but the dusty ranch where my grandmother grew up and the mining claims that my grandfather fruitlessly searched with his father and brothers. But now that we have spent some time in the state, her words have a different meaning. To be from Idaho is to be from the lakes of Stanley Basin, the leafy trees of Boise, the sweet, quiet winds over the Cambridge prairie. It's to be from Boise State University, which published a book on *Trout Fishing in America* as part of its Western Writers Series. It's to be from the hipped-up Modern Hotel with its mid-century swagger, from the restaurants of the Basque Block, from the long, cool Boise River.

I carry my grandmother's home as I carry her bones, the shape of her body, the early silver-gray of her hair. In her casket she wore the bracelets, but before she was buried they were slipped into a blue felt pouch and given to me. Every time I wear them I feel the weight of that ancestry.

⁜

The same year Arline and I went to Idaho, my father's book, *Beyond the Good Death: The Anthropology of Modern Dying*, was published. After we returned from our trip, I sat down and read it. My mind still flickered with images—my grandmother's grave, campsite #4—and my body still carried the rhythm of travel. Something important had happened to me in Idaho, but I couldn't articulate what it was.

In the book, my father wrote about our tendency in the United States, unlike in some other parts of the world, to segregate the sacred from the mundane. We think of the spiritual plane as beyond us, up there in the sky or, even farther, out there in the universe. This is true for those with a more traditional view of Heaven and for those who sense a diffuse cosmic connection but don't call it God.

However, according to scholar Robert A. Orsi—and here I'm paraphrasing my father's paraphrase—our experience of the spiritual is always mediated through the material. We sense the presence of a dead relative as a shiver in our bodies. Or we swell with celestial well-being while listening to a beautiful piece of music. "Religion," Orsi says, "is the practice of making the invisible visible, of concretizing the order of the universe, the nature of human life and its destiny, and the various dimensions and possibilities of human interiority itself." In other words, the only way we can understand life's mysteries—what it means to have a conscious self, whether our lives have meaning, how the universe works—is through the physical world. We make pictures of God. We speak in tongues. We hear voices from beyond. We talk to our ancestors. Religion is this act of transforming abstract mysteries into material realities.

This definition of religion cracked open something inside me. I don't go to church on Sunday or imagine a pleasant afterlife, not even a heavenly picnic where I might reunite with my childhood dog. I'm pretty certain that when I take my last breath, whatever it is that makes me me will dissipate, and that my life has no particular meaning except that I like living it. From time to time as I was growing up, I attended Methodist church with my grandparents. When people in the congregation shuffled up for Communion, I always stayed in the pew, slightly embarrassed but knowing that it would be worse to pretend to believe in the significance of the wafer and wine.

But Orsi's definition suggests that I've been religious all along. When I wear the silver bracelets that clanked when my paternal grandmother came into the room, I am communicating with the dead. When I fill my maternal grandmother's milk-glass chicken with pink and white mints, like she did, I am honoring the dead. Orsi calls these manifestations of a world beyond the material "bearers of sacred presence."

In Ianthe Brautigan's book about her father, she describes a moment where she and her daughter are sitting on the floor looking at papers and posters her father left her, and she realizes that these are the family heirlooms. These bits of his writing, some of which I imagine on napkins and others on elegant letterpressed broadsides, are what bear his presence for her.

Reading my dad's book made me realize that I respond deeply to certain objects, and not only to those associated with my biological ancestors. My pink paperback of *Trout Fishing in America* is a bearer of sacred presence, and I invest it with a meaning that is beyond its material reality. It is the wafer of my communion.

On that beautiful day in September, when Arline and I found the campsite where Brautigan and his family stayed, and I read aloud from *Trout Fishing in America*, I was engaged in what my father calls one of those "small, world-building activities invoking a relationship with whatever cosmic realms and agencies we presuppose, authenticating realities that are imaginatively (if not deductively) real." At Little Redfish Lake I was imagining—and in great detail—the writer and his scenes of inspiration. My religious inclinations, it turns out, go beyond collecting meaningful objects. I will drive six hundred miles to touch the earth trod by a writer.

Now the trip and its significance came into focus. I'd gone to Idaho to invoke a relationship with ancestors both biological and literary. The moments at Big Redfish Lake and at the campsite felt transcendent because they were transcendent. The word *Eucharist*, from Greek, means "thanksgiving," and my journey was a way of giving thanks.

Mayonnaise

Breath

My love for my eighth-grade gym teacher, Mr. Luna, spanned four steno pads. Mr. Luna had been an Olympic gymnast for Ecuador. When I found out he was married, I quoted a Brautigan poem about envy in my steno pad and wrote this poem:

I've been anonymously

sending Richard Brautigan

poems

to him.

Richard Brautigan poems

make me want to write

Richard Brautigan poems.

I guess this is as close as

I'll ever get.

I was not, in fact, sending Mr. Luna Brautigan poems, but at the end of the school year, I gave him a poem about life and death and dreams that had earned an A in my language arts class. He asked politely about my writing and said he usually wrote his poems in Spanish. A day or so later, I lay in wait so he'd have to walk with me down the hall. And on the last day of school, I positioned myself with my steno pad on the edge of the school parking lot so I could watch him drive away. His car dipped into the valley, crested the next hill, and disappeared.

All summer I longed for Mr. Luna, and in the fall, as high school was about to start, I called the middle school to see if he would be working there again. He would not. I went back to the school, where the language arts teacher told me Mr. Luna was working somewhere in the Lake Washington District. This prompted a trip to the library to find the addresses and phone numbers of the schools there. Once high school began, I got too busy to track him down. All of this is documented in the steno pads.

High school began, my new poems became abstract

and inscrutable ("the mist that hides/some truth unknown/ behind the fog/goes on unshown"), and I met the first boy who liked me back, a skinny drummer. My journal entries got longer and more pedestrian, and I started writing fiction. I lamented that I was no longer writing poetry, and that what poems I did write were more essays than poems.

In Steno Pad #15, the drummer and I kissed. Brautigan was never mentioned again.

My solitude ended with that kiss. Pages and pages of fantasies about the one I would love and the one who would love me—most recently, Mr. Luna—gave way to diary entries that parsed actual relationships. But it was Brautigan who'd kept me company during those pre-kiss years. I briefly mentioned e.e. cummings, Kurt Vonnegut, Doris Lessing, and Herman Hesse, but Brautigan's name appeared and re-appeared in the steno pads. I did not research and copy his biographical details, as I did for others I admired. Instead, his words appeared in the notebooks as if they were so ever-present, like water, like air, that they needed no remarking. I was reading him, and his words were in me.

I screwed up. Our first trip to Idaho was launched before I was ready, although I didn't realize it at the time. I returned to Seattle, began working on this manuscript, dug deeper into Brautigan's book, and discovered that I needed to visit Worswick Hot Springs.

In the chapter "Worsewick" (the real name is spelled without the "e"), Brautigan—that is, the *narrator*—sits with his wife in the hot springs and gets an erection. She tells him to pull out before he comes, and he watches his semen mingle with dead fish.

The narrator calls his wife "my woman," which was a popular way to refer to one's wife in the 1960s. But the woman gets no other name in the whole book. His semen gets more description than she does—it's "misty" and "stringy," "like a falling star." The dead fish get more description than she does.

I had to see the location that prompted this cringe-inducing chapter. So, two years after our first trip, I convinced Arline to spend one more week with me in search of another piece of Brautigan's Idaho.

On an August day we head east from Boise toward Mountain Home. The chain restaurants and hotels fall behind us and the ground flattens, soil rooted to earth by pale wheat-colored grasses and sagebrush clumps. The Boise Stage Stop Feed 'n' Fuel says it's eighty-one degrees, and it's not yet ten a.m. Last night in our room at the Modern Hotel in Boise, I read the Worsewick chapter to Arline and asked her how she thought I might have read it as an adolescent. Did I identify with the narrator or his wife? The writer or the muse? Arline said I was missing another dimension: my reading was essentially voyeuristic; I was thirteen and titillated. At that age, she had been hiding Henry Miller's *Tropic of Cancer*. Now, as she steers the car onto Route 20 toward Fairfield, I ask her where she got the copy of Miller and how she hid it. She doesn't remember—perhaps the library, perhaps a friend's house. She and her mother shared a one-bedroom apartment, and her single bed beneath a bookshelf in the dining room was the only space that belonged entirely to her. Maybe she read at night, after her mother had gone to bed.

She's right, of course. I was titillated. Sex was, I knew, an experience in my future, perhaps not too far in my future, and I craved information. Babysitting in various households, I'd found *The Joy of Sex*, *The Story of O*, and Nancy Friday's book of women's sexual fantasies, *My Secret Garden*. The scene of the couple in the hot springs was one more image of what might await. Whether I identified with him or with her would become an interesting question to me as an adult. But at the time, the scene itself was what fascinated me.

I think about this as Route 20 takes us into the Boise National Forest and the foothills of the Soldier Mountains. We're about a hundred miles south of Stanley, where we traveled two years ago, but at a lower elevation. We top a steep hill and a dramatic valley opens below us. A puffball cloud looks comically alone in the blue sky.

I read aloud a chapter, "The Message," that takes place in this area. The narrator and his wife have to wait for a flock of sheep to cross the road. The narrator describes the shepherd as looking like Adolf Hitler but friendly. Arline notes that we saw a sheep-herding wagon in the Basque museum in Boise on our last visit. Maybe the shepherd was Basque.

In Fairfield, Arline pulls up to a caboose that houses the visitor's information center. The woman staffing the center is stretched out on a window seat, sleeping. I tiptoe to the rack of maps, but she wakes up and apologizes. She gives me a Camas County Recreation Map and points us to various options for bathrooms. We opt for the Camas County Public Library down the street. On my way out of the library, I scan the fiction shelves for Brautigan. Nothing. The residents of Camas County live here; they don't need to read Brautigan's account of a couple months on their turf.

Back in the car, pavement turns to dirt and Arline gets apprehensive. The road over Couch Summit, barely wide enough for two cars, switchbacks up the side of the mountain. We come around a corner, the steep drop-off on our right, and a truck pulling a dirt bike on a trailer bears down on us. As the dust settles behind it and we haven't tumbled over the side, she says she was just praying the trailer didn't fishtail.

The road drops into a valley and widens a bit. Now we're hugging Little Smoky Creek in a narrow canyon, making our way toward Worswick Hot Springs. We come upon a slow-moving pickup truck and it pulls over to let us pass. Arline squints at the driver.

I say, "He's just going fishing."

She says, "He's looking at me to decide if he should go fishing or *hunting*."

We're back in the land of Aryans and bears, whether mythical or real.

The bears are, in fact, real, as the notice tacked to the three-paneled wooden sign marking Worswick Hot Springs tells us: DON'T SURPRISE BEARS—MAKE NOISE. Taking no chances, I call up to the three men standing by the lowest pool: "Nice day, huh?" Their fat-tired dirt bikes are splayed along the path. One turns his monumental belly toward me: "Sure is." This does the trick, and they leave us in peace as we survey the scene.

It's not what I had imagined. The hot springs pools of my imagination were tucked into a cozy forest, a private retreat under pines. But these pools are set in an open, denuded hillside, the grasses stamped out by hordes of visitors. An orange tarp lines the lowest pool. Deerflies swarm, but there are no dead fish, and Arline speculates that Brautigan made them up. How would a trout ever wander into a hot spring?

Perhaps when Brautigan visited, the grass still grew to the edges of the pools. He describes no orange tarp, no outhouse, no large wooden sign. Perhaps the spot felt more private. I am surprised but not disappointed. The Soldier Mountains are beautiful, and soon we will wind our way along Little Smoky Creek to the Boise River, making a loop through Featherville and back down to Mountain Home. I wander up the hillside, dipping my fingers in each progressively warmer pool. The hot afternoon doesn't inspire me to change my clothes in the outhouse and soak, not even in the coolest pool at the bottom of the hill.

Now, two years after I stood on the shore of Little Redfish Lake, I realize I have grown more comfortable with my ambivalence about this author who meant so much to me over thirty years ago. Brautigan has become more real, more fully dimensional, in the same way that our parents become more human—that is, more like us—over time. I don't have to come down on one side or the other of him. I can appreciate all of what is *Trout Fishing in America*: its bursts of invention, its troubling passages, its poignancy.

"Darn," I say to Arline as she drives away from Worswick Hot Springs. "If those guys hadn't been there, we could've had sex in one of the pools."

She gives me a look: *not in this lifetime.* Whether what bothers her most is the men and their dirt bikes, the ghost of that stringy semen, or the possibility of elk poop, she is not going to enact some hot lesbian version of Brautigan's scene so I can work it into this book. She refuses even to feel the temperature of the water.

On the trip that started it all, the one that ended at Little Redfish Lake, we had to get back home to teach the fall term, so we didn't follow Brautigan's trail to Lake Josephus. We turned around and drove back the way we had come, through Lowman and Idaho City. It was prettier on the way down than it had been on the way up because we knew where we were and where we were going. Now the campgrounds looked more benign; they weren't sheltering Aryans. Although they may have had bears.

We drove past Meridian, Idaho, where my mother spent some of her early years. We took Highway 95 through Weiser, and I considered calling my brother because we have a joke about Weiser. It's not a hilarious joke. It's mostly just the sound of the name Weiser, like geezer, and we think it'd be funny to be from a place that sounds like that. I didn't call him, though.

In Cambridge, we ate pie at Bucky's and paid respects to my grandparents. My grandfather's name was engraved on the marble slab now, along with his shortwave radio call letters, W7JY. I looked down at the slab and then out at the wheat-brown fields stretching to the horizon. A hot breeze eddied around us. I tried to feel my grandmother's eyes in my eyes, seeing the familiar in that view. Arline waited for me, quiet.

After a while, I introduced Arline to the Tuttles and their botulism tragedy.

Then we had a choice to make. We could go back to I-84 and through Oregon, the way we had come, or we could go north through Lewiston. Not liking to see the same country over again, we headed toward Lewiston.

❉

Riggins, White Bird, Grangeville. These are iconic names to me, places my parents have talked about my whole life. White Bird is where the highway switchbacked so severely that my parents, in their separate childhoods, got sick and their fathers had to pull over the cars. The canyon there is something stunning, the world scooped out by a huge-knuckled hand. Highway 95 runs straight now, but the old highway can be seen weaving back and forth like a drunk.

We got to Lewiston hoping for something sweet and cold. We had to settle for Baskin-Robbins. The quaint old downtown was mostly boarded up; we'd been there seven or eight years before and found a little coffee shop, but now it was gone.

Highway 95 looked like a roundabout way to where we were going, so we took the back highways to Ritzville, Washington. They were smooth, black ribbons through brown fields. Pomeroy, Delaney, Starbuck. We were low on gas and happy to see that station in Starbuck. Three girls sat on a stoop in the distance. I slid the credit card into the slot and pumped the gas. No attendant was attending.

The road sliced through brown desert, panting beneath blue sky. We crossed the Snake River. At one point a car full of young men came up behind us and rode our tail. They detoured off into a tiny campground on the river. It was Friday afternoon. They were having a party.

And then we were alone again. The Snake River met up with the Palouse River. Washtucna, Ralston. We had that same feeling we'd had in Idaho—what if our car broke down? How much water did we have? What if the Aryans found us, or the bears?

We were relieved to see signs of a city on the horizon. Ritzville meant I-90, the highway that would take us home. We pulled onto the interstate and got as far as Moses Lake, but then we had to stop. The oncoming headlights washed across the backs of our eyes, and we knew we shouldn't navigate the mountain passes between here and Puget Sound after fifteen hours on the road. We slept in a cheap motel near the highway. The next morning we were on our way home.

Modern Photography

My first camera was a black box with a scratched window that produced small, square photographs. The time between snapping a picture and holding its white border was at least a few weeks, as each exposure napped in the dark while waiting for the roll to finish.

Now we take pictures, review them on the screen in the camera, delete half of them—if we're not the kind of person who imposes endless slideshows on our friends—and upload them to our computers and websites and email inboxes in a few minutes.

This leaves no time for contemplation.

I have fifty-four images from our trip to Idaho in my computer. I chose seventeen to upload to the Internet and send to family and friends: three of our hotel, one of me in front of the White Savage Apartments in Boise, eight of the Sawtooth Mountains, two of the campsite where Richard Brautigan slept, and three of the cemetery in Cambridge where my grandparents are buried.

Photographs are cheaper now. They don't cost anything to reproduce on our computers. They take up less space because they don't need to be in boxes or photo albums, curling at the edges under yellowing plastic.

By extension, each photograph is less valuable. I have a colleague who occasionally sends me links to her slideshows. They are hundreds of photographs long. I can only watch a dozen or so and then I click away. Maybe the forty-third photograph is the best one, but I never see it.

Still, photographs are not worth nothing. My first profile picture on Facebook was one of the ones taken at campsite #4. I'm standing next to the post with the number, and behind me are the picnic table and the lake. I have just read Brautigan's passage aloud. I am still shivering.

As of this writing, Richard Brautigan has over 25,000 fans on Facebook and over 9,000 people "like" *Trout Fishing in America*. This is not many considering the hundreds of millions of people on the site. But probably most of those hundreds of millions of people were born a generation or two too late to have heard of him. They have their own cult figures that I've never heard of: makers of graphic novels, singers of hip-hop songs, performers of spoken word. We, the collective we, keep right on throwing words up and seeing how they come down, and they keep coming down in new ways that make us sigh.

On Brautigan's Facebook page, someone has posted a woodcut of a mayonnaise jar. It was used as a logo for a library in Vermont modeled after the quirky library in Brautigan's book, *The Abortion*. The label says "Richard's Real Mayonnaise." Apparently the library used mayonnaise jars as bookends. A mayonnaise jar ends *Trout Fishing in America*. What was it about mayonnaise?

What I said before about the nobility of trout frying was a little disingenuous. There's not a lot of poetry to throwing a cast-iron skillet on the stove, oiling it, turning up the gas, waiting for the oil to slick, and throwing in the slimy fish. Much can and usually does go wrong. The skin crackles and burns in the pan, leaving the dishwasher—usually the same person as the trout fryer—with a crummy job later. The outer flesh flakes and oozes white scum while the inner flesh stubbornly holds on to its gelatinous pinkness. The entire tail dries out. Nothing changes the essentially bland taste, and what looks like an innocent meal is riddled with bones.

The rituals that accompany the frying and serving can be just as challenging to execute. These begin long before the fish hits the pan. The moment the trout fisher arrives home, the trout fryer is expected to begin an appreciative chant. The content of this chant varies, but it always includes references to the length and girth of the fish (and there may be more than one). The fryer nods, widens her eyes, and makes ritualized noises that punctuate the fisher's story of how this particular fish came to be lying in this particular cooler. The chanting and vocalizing wanes and waxes over several hours, depending on how long before dinner the fisher arrives.

Once the fish is on the counter and the pan heating, the call-and-response picks up again as the fisher retells fragments of the story and the fryer responds as if she has never heard them before. There is a pause as the skin seizes in the oil; water droplets explode like firecrackers. The fryer closes her mouth to concentrate on the fish while tossing the salad, slicing the bread, and unwrapping a block of butter and dropping it onto a plate. The fisher twists a corkscrew into a bottle of wine.

The carrying of salad, bread, wine, and butter to the table is done without ceremony, but all eyes are upon the platter of fish as the fryer—or sometimes the fisher—brings it to the table. In some households this moment is accompanied by a respectful silence; in others, there may be a series of moans or audible exhalations of breath. Often, when the platter is set on the table, the participants clap, marking the turn from solemnity to celebration. This is followed by a more or less silent period while the participants dish out, pass, pour, and begin to eat. After about ten minutes, the fisher praises the fryer, who denies having done anything out of the ordinary, and then comments on the difference between the fish when it was alive and fighting his hook and as it is now, subdued and cooling. The ritual is now complete. And as it is with all rituals, someone cleans up afterwards.

The truth is, trout's not my thing. I prefer salmon. When king salmon from Alaska start coming to town, I buy a fat fillet and drizzle it with olive oil. The best salmon doesn't need more than that. Throw it on the grill for about ten minutes. Let it sit a few more. The flesh melts pink.

Later in the season, sockeye is almost as good. If it looks iffy, make a sauce. Fry the salmon, skin-side down, in a cast-iron skillet. Whisk together miso, mirin, chopped garlic and ginger, rice vinegar, and soy sauce. When the salmon's done, lift it from the pan, pour in the sauce, scrape up the bits of skin, and let the sauce reduce. Pour it over the salmon and sprinkle with chopped scallions.

I don't know how to fish. I don't even know how they catch wild salmon these days. But as long as they do—as long as the salmon run—I'll be cooking it every summer. Arline walks over to the bakery for a baguette, and I toss a salad of vegetables from the farmer's market. While the salmon is grilling, she uncorks a bottle of local wine. We take our plates and wine glasses to the back patio, and while the dog tempts us to throw his ball, we share the meal.

The Last 177.65 Miles

The last 177.65 miles of our trip from Seattle to Boise to Stanley to Cambridge to Seattle was from Moses Lake to our house. MapQuest says it should have taken us two hours and forty-nine minutes but I'm absolutely sure it took us no more than two hours and forty minutes because I was driving pretty fast that late-summer morning, and the sun was behind us instead of in our eyes, and it floated up into the cool blue sky and followed us all the way home.

I wish I could sing now the song of that drive home, a drive I have taken so many, many times that the towns are like the lines of an old song that always makes me feel both sweet and melancholy. A song like "Lean on Me" or "Sitting on the Dock of the Bay." The words go like this: "George, Vantage, Ellensburg, Thorp, Cle Elum, Snoqualmie Pass, North Bend, Issaquah, Bellevue, Seattle." Everyone in the car starts singing the song together, and it reminds us that we do have something in common with other people, that there is a common language for the important moments in a life, that there is a ritual, a ceremony, and we're not lost, isolated beings having to make everything up on our own as we go along. It reminds us of our religion.

Arline and I sang the going-home song all the way home, and the desert turned to foothills and the foothills turned to mountains and we went up, up, up, and down the other side, speeding through the pass so green and easy this time of year. Forest gave way to suburb, suburb crammed into city, and soon we were driving over the Lake Washington Bridge and into the tunnel and onto the exit for southbound Rainier Avenue, and then we were on our very own Rainier Avenue, the artery we take in and out of the city's heart. It was almost as if we had just gone out for coffee; we were on the same streets we drove every day. We passed the grocery store and the hardware store and the new light-rail station they were building. We passed the taco truck and the nail shops and the food bank. We hung a right at Golden Auto Glass and turned left past Bill's house and Andy's house and the house where they used to have the pit bull-lab mix that terrorized the neighborhood. We turned onto our street, and when we pushed the button for the garage door, it creaked open and we were sailing in. The garden was still green.

Cutthroat Trout Earn Their Name

Here's the hopeful thing: all over Seattle—all over the world—there's a movement afoot to "daylight" streams. Creeks and rivers and streams that were funneled into pipes and sewer systems as houses took all available land are being let loose from their prisons and allowed to see daylight again. Pipers Creek in Seattle, buried by the railroad in the late nineteenth century, was daylighted recently, and chum salmon were reintroduced. One kind of fish didn't need reintroducing. It'd managed to survive all those years of darkness: cutthroat trout. The Washington Department of Fish and Wildlife calls it, grandly, the "ancestral, resident cutthroat trout population."

Imagine those bad years, when the trains shook and clattered above, and the walls of their home narrowed to a culvert under the tracks. The last salmon spawned in the creek in 1927, and their children didn't come back. It was like those small towns where the kids went away to college and forgot about their old parents. The trout threw so many bon voyage parties for the salmon that they got sick of onion dip.

During storms, the creek filled with the slimy waste of their neighbors—motor oil, dog poop, cigarette butts. Some of the trout survived on the serotonin reuptake inhibitors released from human urine. Others responded to the rampant stereotypes about them and got more cutthroat than cutthroat usually are.

Even now, the salmon get all the attention. Every year as part of Earth Day, chum salmon fingerlings are introduced into Pipers Creek, and people come from all over the city to see. The cutthroat roll their watery eyes at each other. They spawn, too, you know. Their fingerlings adorably swish their tails, too, and no one needs to hand-carry them from the Suquamish Tribe's hatchery to Carkeek Park. But that's humans for you. First they practically suffocate you under their trains, then they come back saying they're all sorry and they'll never do it again, but inevitably their attention wanders.

Brautigan didn't make it to his fifties. But the cutthroat trout keep right on living. As long as there's water.

Epilogue

The woman on the cover of *Trout Fishing in America* is Michaela Clark LeGrand. In October 2010, Arline and I stood before a large print of the cover photograph, on display for a celebration of the opening of the Brautigan Library at the Clark County Historical Museum in Vancouver, Washington. In this print, ten times larger than the book cover, LeGrand looked more knowing than I'd given her credit for. According to Jen, who blogs at *The Brautigan Pages*, the photograph was a last-minute idea of the photographer, Erik Weber. So Brautigan didn't have a chance to mention LeGrand in his sly, self-referential opening chapter. How convenient of me to ignore logistics and find evidence for Brautigan's misogyny (blah, blah, blah) in her absence from his text.

How convenient of me, as well, to conjure my own Richard Brautigan out of his books and my imagination. At the celebration in Vancouver, I would come as close as possible to the actual Brautigan. Dr. John Barber, who organized the celebration, had brought Brautigan's daughter Ianthe to speak. About fifty celebrants gathered in a brick-lined room of the museum to hear Barber's introduction to the author. Then Ianthe stepped up to the podium. I looked for evidence of the writer in her face, but having never known him, I could only see that she was tall, with gold-brown hair and open, green eyes. She told a funny story of teenagers plagiarizing Brautigan and winning writing awards in their high schools. She said he would have loved the library.

Afterwards, I asked her about the Idaho trip, and she said she didn't remember it. Arline asked who changed her diapers on the trip, and she said her parents hadn't worried much about diapers; she ran around in a scarf half the time.

For the celebration, someone had made a life-size cutout of Brautigan from the *Trout Fishing in America* cover. He stood with his hands in the pockets of his peacoat, slouchy hat pulled down to his eyes. Arline took a picture of me next to it, hands in my pockets, mimicking his stance. Meeting Ianthe and posing with the cutout were as close to flesh-and-blood Brautigan as I'd ever get, and yet the man I'd followed through Idaho is almost as real to me as my own grandparents.

But isn't that what readers do? We conjure our own writers of the books we love. We travel with them, argue with them, kiss them, turn away from them only to turn back and sigh in nostalgia over what they—and we—once were. And isn't that what we writers want? To drape the bracelets of our presence around our readers' wrists? To bump against the bones of their hands?

That pink-covered paperback, more worn than when I started this project, will stay with me forever. Even as I clean out my closets and shelves, I will always keep this book, in the same way that I will always keep the milk-glass chicken and the silver bracelets of my grandmothers. The book will always reflect back the me that was and the me I am now.

"A Nostalgic Morning"

"I read in the travel section"
Rusha Haljuci, "Three Books that Will Take You Back on the Road," *New York Times*, March 23, 2008.

"a slim pink paperback"
My copy of *Trout Fishing in America* is a Dell Laurel Edition dated February 1972.

"the Brautigan archives"
The Richard Brautigan archives are at
http://brautigan.cybernetic-meadows.net.

"Orienteering"
"John Barber's online Brautigan archives"
John F. Barber's Brautigan site is at http://www.brautigan.net.

"My Parents' Record Collection"

"A Pew Research Center survey"
Paul Taylor and Rich Morin, "Forty Years after Woodstock: A Gentler Generation Gap," August 12, 2009, http://www.pewsocialtrends.org/2009/08/12/forty-years-after-woodstockbra-gentler-genera-tion-gap/.

"After Stonewall, Before Ellen"

"Like someone named Karen"
The online comment from Karen, dated April 18, 2008, appears at thenewgay.net/2008/04/can-queer-girls-have-boyfriends.html.

"Meanwhile in Panama"

"El Día de los Mártires"
Arline supplied most of the details about the events in Panama in 1964; I found additional information from a narrative by Eric Jackson, editor of The Panama News:
http://www.czbrats.com/Jackson/martyrs/martyrs.htm.

"A Route"

"William Hjortsberg's biography of Brautigan"
William Hjortsberg, *Jubilee Hitchhiker: The Life and Times of Richard Brautigan* (Counterpoint Press, 2012).

"The Woman Who Travels with Him"

"According to web sources"
Information in this chapter is from John F. Barber's site and Bigislandchronicle.com.

"The Baby Who Travels with Him"

"You Can't Catch Death"
Ianthe Brautigan, *You Can't Catch Death: A Daughter's Memoir* (St. Martin's Griffin, 2001).

"Brautigan + Misogyny = Blah, Blah, Blah"

"Brautigan's view of women has a tad of schoolboy misogyny about it, but benignly so."
Jill Murphy's comment is in a review of *Revenge of the Lawn* on The Bookbag, http://www.thebookbag.co.uk/reviews/index.php?title=Revenge_of_the_Lawn_by_Richard_Brautigan.

"Brautigan, kind of a misogynist, but we loves him so."
Alex Carnevale's comment is from a Tumblr blog: http://thisrecording.tumblr.com/post/43064256/brautigan-kind-of-a-misogynist-but-we-loves-him.

"Mild undertone of casual misogyny."
The comment from Kedves is no longer online.

"He can do no wrong (apart from the whiffs of misogyny that I can try to pretend are 'of the era')."
The comment from Caro is no longer online.

"So we all know in class how Brautigan was accused of being misogynistic, egotistical, blah blah blah."
Molly Vogel wrote in a blog post for a class: http://mollyvogel.blogspot.com/2008/10/i-dont-want-my-daughter-to-be-educated.html.

"And Still the Girls will Read the Boys and the Boys Won't Read the Girls"

"The Harry Potter phenomenon exemplifies what research has definitively shown"
See, for example, Elizabeth Dutro, "But That's a Girls' Book!' Exploring Gender Boundaries in Children's Reading Practices," *Reading Teacher*, Vol. 55, No. 4 (2001): 376.

"Shivering"

"The Teddy Roosevelt Chingader'"
As far as I can tell, the word "chingader' " is from "chingadera," Spanish slang for, roughly, "fucking thing." Since the italicized note at the beginning of the chapter says that the Challis National Forest was created by Roosevelt, the title seems to be referring to the forest as the thing which is fucked.

"The Mysterious Beyond"

"Mrs. George Hall Answers the Final Call to the Mysterious Beyond"
The obituary appeared in what is now called the *Upper Country News-Reporter*.

"My Inner Trout"

"*Downstream from Trout Fishing in America*"
Keith Abbot, *Downstream from Trout Fishing in America* (Capra Press, 1989).

"What the Scholars Tell Us"

"One scholar, from the 1970s, says the theme of *Trout* is escape into the imagination, now that escape into the wilderness is no longer possible"
"Escape through Imagination in *Trout Fishing in America*," Thomas Hearron, *Critique*, 16:1, 1974

"Another says it's that the real America is far from the ideal America of our imaginations."
David L. Vanderwerken, "*Trout Fishing in America* and the American Tradition," *Critique*, 16:1, 1974

"A third, from the 1980s, says it's the triumph of art over death."

Brooke Horvath, "Richard Brautigan's Search for Control over Death," *American Literature*, 57:3, October 1985.

"A Girl from Idaho"

"Boise State University, which published a book on *Trout Fishing in America* as part of its Western Writers Series."
Joseph Mills, Reading *Richard Brautigan's Trout Fishing in America*, 1998.

"Beyond the Good Death: The Anthropology of Modern Dying."
James Green, *Beyond the Good Death: The Anthropology of Modern Dying* (University of Pennsylvania Press, 2008).

The quotations from Robert A. Orsi originally appeared in *Between Heaven and Earth: The Religious Worlds People Make and the Scholars Who Study Them* (Princeton University Press, 2005).

ACKNOWLEDGEMENTS

These organizations generously gave me time and space to write: Soapstone, Hedgebrook, The Jack Straw Writers Program, The Helen Riaboff Whiteley Center, and Highline College. A Seattle Office of Arts and Cultural Affairs CityArtist grant allowed me to complete a draft of the manuscript.

Dinty W. Moore and workshop participants critiqued the early chapters at the Creative Nonfiction Writers' Conference in Oxford, Mississippi.

My writing group has helped me keep the faith: Alma García, Donna Miscolta, and Jennifer D. Munro. This book wouldn't exist without their smart, honest feedback and support.

The team at Ooligan Press has been a writer's dream come true: Abbey Gaterud, Brian Tibbetts, Sabrina Parys, Tenaya Mulvihill, Ryan Brewer, Katey Trnka, Brooke Horn, Geoff Wallace, Missy Lacock, Emily Goldman, Corinne Gould, Brian Parker, Kristin Choruby, Sophie Aschwanden, Erika Schnatz, Meaghan Corwin, Ariana Vives, and Zach Eggemeyer. I can't gush enough about project manager Ariana Marquis, who has handled the process with professionalism and grace.

My parents, James and Carol Green, gave me books, miles of roads, and the confidence to write.

Arline García is the woman who travels with me. I am so grateful.

Photo by Sean Young

Allison Green lives in Seattle, Washington, where she teaches at Highline College. She earned an MFA from Emerson College. She is the author of *Half-Moon Scar* (published by St. Martin's Press) and has also had her writing published by *Gettysburg Review*, *Calyx*, *Bellingham Review*, *Defunct*, *Zyzzyva*, *Yes! Magazine*, *The Common*, *Jumpstart*, *Raven Chronicles*, *Willow Springs*, *Teacher's Voice*, and *Evergreen Chronicles*. The city of Seattle awarded her a CityArtist grant in 2010.

Ooligan Press

Ooligan Press is a general trade publisher rooted in the rich literary tradition of the Pacific Northwest. Ooligan strives to discover works that reflect the diverse values and rich cultures that inspire so many to call the region their home. Founded in 2001, the press is a vibrant and integral part of Portland's publishing community, operating within the Department of English at Portland State University. Ooligan Press is staffed by graduate students working under the guidance of a core faculty of publishing professionals.

Project Manager
Ariana Marquis

Acquisitions
Brian Tibbetts (manager)
Sabrina Parys (manager)
Tenaya Mulvihill (manager)
Meagan Lobnitz

Editing
Katey Trnka (manager)
Melissa Gifford
Emily Goldman
Brooke Horn
Missy Lacock
Geoff Wallace

Design
Erika Schnatz (manager)
Ryan Brewer
Meaghan Corwin
Zach Eggemeyer

Digital
Meaghan Corwin (manager)
Emily Goldman
Corinne Gould
Missy Lacock

Marketing
Ariana Vives (manager)
Sophie Aschwanden
Ryan Brewer
Kristen Choruby
Zach Eggemeyer
Melissa Gifford
Emily Goldman
Corinne Gould
Brooke Horn
Missy Lacock
Brian Parker
Katey Trnka
Geoff Wallace

The Ghosts That Travel with Me is set in Alegreya ht,
designed by Juan Pablo del Peral for Huerta Tipográfica.

CPSIA information can be obtained at www.ICGtesting.com
Printed in the USA
BVOW08s1611170515

400496BV00002B/2/P